THE
MUNRO
ALMANAC

Cameron McNeish

Neil Wilson Publishing • Glasgow • Scotland

© Cameron McNeish, 1996

Published by Neil Wilson Publishing Ltd
303a The Pentagon Centre
36 Washington St
Glasgow G3 8AZ
Scotland
Tel: 0141-221-1117
Fax: 0141-221-5363

A catalogue record for this book is available from
the British Library

ISBN 1-897784-39-2

Typeset in 9 on 9½pt Bodoni by The Write Stuff,
Glasgow. Tel: 0141 339 8279.
E-mail: *wilson_i@cqm.co.uk*

Printed in the United Arab Emirates
by Oriental Press

Contents

Introduction

The Munros are the separate mountains over 3000 feet in Scotland. This book describes 277 such mountains, the 276 as contained in the 1981 edition of *Munro's Tables* (published by the Scottish Mountaineering Trust) plus the addition of Beinn Teallach in 1984.

Periodic revisions have taken place ever since Sir Hugh T. Munro, Bart, of Lindertis published his original list in 1891. In that list, published in the *Scottish Mountaineering Club Journal*, he claimed 538 tops over 3000 feet, 283 of which he believed merited status as 'separate mountains'. There has always been much speculation about the criteria for deciding what separates a 'top' from a 'mountain'. In 1933, J. Gall Inglis, then editor of *Munro's Tables*, suggested that there should be a drop of 75-100 feet between mountains but to date there has been no firm guideline on what constitutes a 'mountain'. Munro himself was in favour of updating only when maps were resurveyed and revised.

But almost immediately, the Ordnance Survey (OS) published their revised six-inch maps of Scotland and discrepancies were found in Munro's tabulations. Munro himself began a revision of his list but sadly died in 1919, aged 63, before it was published. J.R. Young and A.W. Peacock, fellow members of the Scottish Mountaineering Club (SMC), took on the task and working from Munro's notes and card index eventually produced a revised *Munro's Tables* in 1921. This new list produced 276 separate mountains of over 3000 feet.

Various committees and editors of *Munro's Tables* have made alterations to the list since, based mainly on new surveys. Such alterations have not always gone without criticism. There is a strong lobby which insists that the *Munro's Tables* should remain faithful to the historical document which Sir Hugh Munro compiled, while others are happy to go along with the various additions and deletions which are thrown up now and again by the

Ordnance Survey. However, a major revision took place in 1981 at the hands of Hamish Brown and J.C. Donaldson when 47 of Munro's 'tops' were demoted and seven 'mountains' were dropped to 'top' status. In addition 22 new 'tops' were introduced and four 'tops' were promoted to 'mountain' status. This created some controversy at the time with one writer claiming that the changes had been made 'solely at the whim of the editors'. It was felt that perhaps Munro would turn in his grave, as Carn Cloich-mhuillin in the Cairngorms, the mountain which he hoped to climb as his final 3000-footer, had been demoted in the 'incomprehensible' Brown/Donaldson revisions.

But such are the emotions stirred by the Munros. In 1974 metrication was adopted and metric heights appeared side by side with the more familiar imperial heights, but in the 1981 revision the imperial figures were removed. This also caused some consternation and there were fears that the Munros would be considered as those mountains which reached the 1000-metre plumbline, rather than 3000 feet. These fears were proved false but there is still a reluctance to refer to a Munro as 'a mountain of over 914 metres'.

Sir Hugh Munro never completed his round, he died before climbing the Inaccessible Pinnacle in the Cuillin of Skye and Carn Cloich-mhuillin, mentioned above. In 1901 the Revd. A.E. Robertson completed the first ascent of all 283 mountains and another cleric, the Revd. A.R.G. Burn became the first person to climb all the Munros and 'tops' in 1923.

Surprisingly in view of the numbers crawling round the Munros today, it wasn't until 1971 that the number of Munroists (those who have climbed all the 3000-feet 'mountains') reached 100. Hundreds more have become members of this once élite band and today the activity known as 'Munro-bagging' is a popular and growing aspect of Scottish mountaineering.

The Scottish Mountaineering Club keep a list of those who have 'compleated' (sic) the round of Munros and the present 'keeper' of those records is Dr. C.M. Huntley, Old Medwyn, Spittal, Carnwath, Lanarkshire ML11 8LY. While the SMC doesn't officially keep 'records' of the quickest rounds, the fastest to date goes to Andrew Johnstone and Rory Gibson in 1992 who climbed all 277 Munros in a remarkable 51 days! In 1974 Hamish Brown became the first person to climb all the mountains in one expedition and in 1979 Kathy Murtgatroyd became the first woman to climb them all in a similar fashion. In 1984-85, Martin Moran climbed them all during the months of the winter equinox. They have been climbed on mountain bike, (or while carrying a mountain bike) and others have attempted to climb them all on skis. To date no less than 16 individuals have climbed the Munros in a single expedition.

NOTES ON USING THIS BOOK

While the *Munro's Tables* offer lists of the Munros and the 'tops', not to forget the Corbetts, those hills which reach the 2500-feet contour and the *Donald's Tables* of those lowland hills which top 2000 feet; and while other guide books, including the *Munro's Tables* companion volume, The Munros, offer details of the routes on the mountains, I wanted to put together a work which offered as much information as possible about the Munros in one small book.

Each section contains information on accommodation, public transport to and within the section area, the height and grid reference of each summit, the meaning and pronunciation of each mountain and details of the most straightforward ascent, including approximate times, distances and ascent climbed.

Contour line measurements in the route description are given in metres in line with the most recent 1:50 000 Ordnance Survey (OS) maps. For distances on the hill both miles and kilometres are quoted as well as feet and metres as appropriate.

The route descriptions [🐾] are not meant to give a step by step account of how to climb the mountain, but only a very rough outline of what I have found to be the best route of ascent. Many will disagree with some of the recommended routes, but I have tried to balance the need for longer multi-top expeditions with shorter day trips. No one climbs the Munros at the rate of one mountain per day, and there is a great satisfaction to be had in walking the likes of the South Glen Shiel Ridge when you can traverse seven Munros in a day. Likewise there will be those capable of walking the likes of the Cuillin Ridge in one day, while I have broken it up into four expeditions.

These descriptions should only be used as a guide, in conjunction with the appropriate Ordnance Survey (OS) map.

ACCESS

It has always been understood that in Scotland the hillwalker or mountaineer has enjoyed a moral right of 'freedom to roam' in wild places, provided that is accompanied by good countryside manners and respect for those other activities which are undertaken in wild areas, such as grouse shooting and deer stalking [🦌]. This de facto freedom to roam must be safeguarded, for sadly there is a growing number of landowners who are worried about the increased numbers of walkers on the hills and who are anxious to see a change in the law regarding access. In short, the law at present says a trespass has been committed by a person who goes on to land owned or occupied by another without that person's consent and without having a right to do so. But a simple trespass is not enshrined in statute as a criminal offence, so there can't be a prosecution. The owner or occupier of the property must either obtain interdict, (i.e. a court ruling that the trespass must not happen again), or, if damage to property has occurred, to raise an action for damages. Additionally, a 'trespasser' may be asked by the owner or occupier to leave the property and in the event of that person refusing to leave, the owner or occupier has the right to use 'reasonable force' to make him or her leave. There is no further definition as regards 'reasonable force'.

However, there is a widely held public acceptance that walkers and climbers are more or less free to roam the upland areas of Scotland without undue restriction, and any impingement on that 'moral right' would undoubtedly create public outcry. Most estates in the Highlands are involved in deer stalking and ask hillwalkers to respect the stag-shooting season which runs from 20 August to

20 October. During this time there are many areas which are not affected by stalking, like those owned by the National Trust for Scotland (NTS) and many Scottish Natural Heritage (SNH) reserves. I have listed local telephone numbers of estates, however, so that you can find out for yourself where stalking is taking place. Often a chat with the gamekeeper or factor will result in a good compromise with the shooters chasing their deer on one side of the estate and the Munro-bagger enjoying his or her walk on the other.

Bear in mind that estates earn a large part of their annual income from stalking, and there often has to be compromise. The alternative to stalking on many estates could well be something more unpleasant, like mass conifer afforestation.

Following a long-running consultation process by Scottish Natural Heritage, a document, *Scotland's Hills and Mountains — Concordat on Access*, was duly agreed in January 1996 by representatives of the main organisations involved in landowning, farming and recreational use of the Scottish hills.

The Concordat recognises the longstanding tradition of access to hill land in Scotland and provides a framework for a common understanding between landowners. In short, the Concordat encourages responsible access and aims to ensure that people can continue to enjoy access to the open hill in a way which shows consideration for the interests of others. It's a document that has been greatly welcomed and shows that the only way forward is by mutual respect and understanding.

Cameron McNeish
Newtonmore
January 1996

1   BEN LOMOND AND THE ARROCHAR ALPS

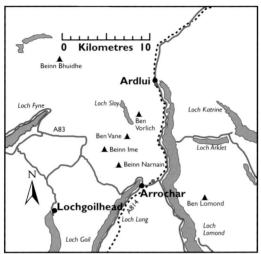

Suggested Base	Arrochar
Accommodation	Hotels, guest houses and b/b at Arrochar, Ardlui, Cairndow, Inveraray, Lochgoilhead and Tarbet. Youth Hostels at Arrochar (Ardgarten), Balloch, Inverarary, Inverbeg and Rowardennan. Camping/caravan sites at Ardgarten, Ardlui, Arrochar, Balloch, Balmaha, Inveraray and Luss.
Public Transport	Rail: London to Fort William and Glasgow to Oban and Fort William. Stations at Arrochar and Ardlui. There is also a train line from Glasgow to Balloch on Loch Lomondside. Buses: Balmaha, Arrochar, Glen Croe, Glen Kinglas, Cairndow, Loch Shira and Aberfoyle can all be reached by bus from Glasgow.

BEN LOMOND, 3195FT/974M

Map: OS Sheet 56: GR 367029
Translation: beacon hill
Pronunciation: low-mond
Access Point: Rowardennan Hotel, GR 360983
Distance/ascent: 7mls/3195ft; 11km/974m
Approx Time: 4-6 hours

🏃 Follow path through trees from Rowardennan Hotel to lower slopes of south ridge. Follow obvious path along broad middle ridge to summit cone where the path zig-zags to summit ridge. A few bumps in the ridge lead to the summit.

🦌 National Trust for Scotland. No restrictions.

BEINN NARNAIN, 3038FT/926M
BEINN IME, 3316FT/1011M

Map: OS Sheet 56: GR 272067 and GR 255085
Translation: unknown and butter hill
Pronunciation: byn naar-nain, byn eem
Access Point: A83 at Loch Long, GR 294050
Distance/ascent: 7mls/4000ft; 11km/1219m
Approx Time: 5-7 hours

Beinn Narnain from the slopes of Beinn Ime

🏃 Start near turn off to Succoth Farm. Follow path steeply uphill through forest to open hill. Continue NW up broad ridge to the knoll of

Cruach nam Miseag. Follow faint path through rock to the Spearhead, a rock prow which lies on the ridge. Climb a short gully on its right to summit plateau of Beinn Narnain. Continue to Beinn Ime by way of Bealach a'Mhaim then climb NNW slopes to summit trig point.

🦌 No restrictions.

BEN VANE, 3002FT/915M

Map: OS Sheet 56: GR 278098
Translation: middle hill
Pronunciation: as spelt
Access Point: Inveruglas, Loch Lomondside, GR 322099
Distance/ascent: 7mls/3000ft; 11km/914m
Approx Time: 4-6 hours

🚶 Follow Hydro Board track to Coiregrogain for just over a mile and then take the ESE ridge of the hill. Higher up the ridge you'll have to thread your way through some rocky and slabby outcrops, but there should be no real difficulty.

🦌 No restrictions. NB: Parking at the foot of the Hydro Board road is discouraged. Park opposite Loch Sloy Power Station to the north.

BEN VORLICH, 3094FT/943M

Map: OS Sheets 56 and 50: GR 295124
Translation: hill of the bay
Pronunciation: as spelt
Access Point: Ardlui Station, GR 318154
Distance/ascent: 6mls/3020ft; 10km/902m
Approx Time: 4-6 hours

🚶 Take the second railway underpass to the south of Ardlui Station and then take heather slopes to Coire Creagach. Climb on the NW side of the stream to the upper corrie where the main ridge will be reached NNE of the summit.

🦌 No restrictions.

BEINN BHUIDHE, 3110FT/948M

Map: OS Sheet 50: GR 204187
Translation: yellow hill
Pronunciation: byn voo-ie
Access Point: Glen Fyne, GR 228160
Distance/ascent: 6mls/3100ft; 10km/945m
Approx Time: 5-7 hours

🦌 Park in the loop road between the A83 and the
old Fyne bridge. Vehicles are not allowed to
drive up the Glen Fyne road unless they are on
official business, although bicycles are allowed
provided they keep to the road. Walk up Glen
Fyne to Inverorachan, then take to the slopes
due west. Follow the south bank of the stream
to its source then bear NW up steep grass and
bracken into the upper corrie. Climb one of the
gullies to the ridge. The summit cone is about
halfway along the ridge.

🦌 Ardkinglas Estate Office. Tel: 01499-600217.

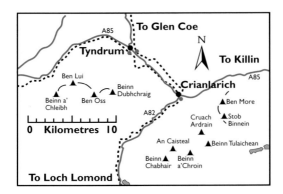

Suggested Base	Crianlarich
Accommodation	Hotels, guest houses and b/b at Crianlarich and Tyndrum. Youth Hostel at Crianlarich. Caravan site at Tyndrum and camping/caravan site in Glendochart.
Public Transport	Rail: Crianlarich and Tyndrum are on the West Highland Line, London/Glasgow to Fort William. Also Glasgow to Oban line. Buses: Glasgow to Fort William or Oban for Crianlarich or Tyndrum.

BEINN CHABHAIR, 3061FT/933M

Map: OS Sheets 50 and 56: GR 367180
Translation: possibly hill of the hawk
Pronunciation: byn chavaar
Access Point: Beinglas, GR 319188
Distance/ascent: 8mls/2850ft; 13km/869m
Approx Time: 4-5 hours

ᴙ Climb steeply behind Beinglas Farm to above
the falls of the Ben Glas Burn. Follow the burn
to Lochan Beinn Chabhair then climb

diagonally NE to the NW ridge. Follow ridge to summit.

🦌 Glen Falloch Estate. Tel: 01301-704229.

AN CAISTEAL, 3264FT/995M
BEINN A'CHROIN, 3084FT/940M

Map: OS Sheets 50 and 56: GR 379193 and
    GR 394186
Translation: the castle; hill of danger
Pronunciation: an casteel; byn a kroin
Access Point: Glen Falloch, GR 368238
Distance/ascent: 9mls/2600ft; 14km/792m
Approx Time: 4-6 hours

🚶 Follow rough track under railway, over the
river by a bridge and up its west bank. Climb
slopes of Sron Garbh and follow the ridge,
Twistin' Hill to An Caisteal. Descent SSE ridge
to col and climb rocky NW end of Beinn
a'Chroin's summit ridge. Continue along crest
to summit.

🦌 Glen Falloch Estate. Tel: 01301-704229.

CRUACH ARDRAIN, 3431FT/1046M
BEINN TULAICHEAN, 3104FT/946M

Map: OS Sheets: 50,51,56 and 57: GR 409211 and
    GR 416196
Translation: stack of the high part; hill of the
    hillocks
Pronunciation: kroo-ach ardrain; byn too-leach-
    an
Access Point: A82 road just south of Crianlarich,
    GR 382245
Distance/ascent: 9mls/3500ft; 14km/1067m
Approx Time: 5-7 hours

🚶 Cross bridge over railway to gain access to
forest. Go right, then left through a large
clearing following a path. Reach a broken fence
after a short distance, go uphill following the
fence posts until you reach the open hillside.
Turn SE up the NW ridge to Grey Height, then
Meall Dhamh. Follow path downhill, across a
col and then steeply up to Cruach Ardrain. To

continue south to Tulaichean return SW past
two cairns and descend to a grassy ridge.
Follow crest of this ridge south to Beinn
Tulaichean.

🦌 No restrictions. NB: Beinn Tulaichean can also
be climbed from Inverlochlarig in the south.

BEN MORE, 3852FT/1174M
STOB BINNEIN, 3822FT/1165M

Map: OS Sheet 51: GR 432244 and GR 434226
Translation: big hill; hill of the anvil
Pronunciation: stobinyan
Access Point: Benmore Farm, GR 414257
Distance/ascent: 9mls/5165ft; 14km/1574m
Approx Time: 6-8 hours

🐾 Leave the farm and bear right towards the
ridge of Sron nam Forsairean. Follow this to
the summit. A hanging corrie, immediately
below the summit facing NW has a steep upper
section which is liable to avalanche in snowy
conditions. This is the site of several fatalities
so avoid it if you can. Descend south from Ben
More, then SW following an indistinct ridge to
the flat Bealach-eader-dha Beinn. Climb Stob
Binnein from here by its north ridge.

🦌 Tel: 01838-306281

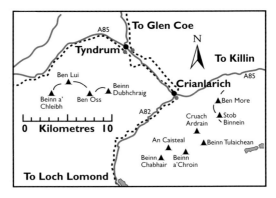

Suggested Base   Tyndrum
Accommodation   Hotels, guest houses and b/b in
          Tyndrum, Crianlarich and
          Bridge of Orchy. Youth Hostel
          at Crianlarich and private bunk
          house at Bridge of Orchy.
          Caravan site at Tyndrum.
Public Transport   Rail: Tyndrum is on West
          Highland Line, London to Fort
          William, and the Glasgow-Oban
          line. Buses: Glasgow to Fort
          William or Glasgow to Oban.

BEINN A'CHLEIBH, 3005FT/916M
BEN LUI, 3707FT/1130M

Map: OS Sheet 50: GR 251256, GR 266263
Translation: hill of the crest; hill of the calf
Pronunciation: *chlayv*; *loo-ie*
Access Point: Glen Lochay, GR 239278
Distance/ascent: 7mls/3300ft; 11km/1006m
Approx Time: 4-7 hours

Start at access point and cross River Lochay by
   stepping stones. Follow path on the east side of
   the Eas Daimh through conifer forest. After
   quarter of a mile cross the burn and follow the

path to the stile in the fence which leads to open hillside. Climb NNW ridge of Ben Lui to summit. Descend SW to the bealach at the head of Fionn Choirein and follow flat ridge to the summit of Beinn a'Chleibh.

🦌 Forestry Commission. Tel: 01546-602518.

BEN OSS, 3373FT/1028M
BEINN DUBHCRAIG, 3205FT/977M

Map: OS Sheet 50: GR 287253, GR 308255
Translation: loch outlet hill; black rock hill
Pronunciation: doo-craig
Access Point: Dailrigh, GR 344290
Distance/ascent: 12mls/3300ft; 19km/1006m
Approx Time: 4-7 hours

🐾 Leave Dailrigh in Strathfillan. Follow rough road on south side of river to a bridge over the railway. Head west and cross the Allt Coire Dubhcraig. Follow path through woods to open hillside and continue SW up grassy corrie to the shoulder of Beinn Dubhcraig. Follow broad stony ridge to summit. From Dubhcraig follow ridge NW and W to Ben Oss.

🦌 Glen Falloch Estate. Tel: 01301-704229.

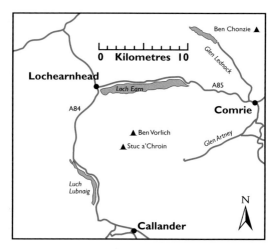

Ben Chonzie ▲

Glen Lednock

Lochearnhead

A85

Loch Earn

Comrie

A84

▲ Ben Vorlich

Glen Artney

▲ Stuc a'Chroin

Luch
Lubnaig

N

Callander

0 **Kilometres** 10

Suggested Base	St Fillans or Comrie
Accommodation	Hotels, guest houses and b/b at Callander, Comrie, Crieff, Lochearnhead, St. Fillans and Strathyre. Camping sites at Callander and Crieff. Caravan/camping at Comrie.
Public Transport	Rail: London, Glasgow and Edinburgh to Inverness. Connecting buses from stations at Perth and Stirling. Buses: Stirling to Crieff for ongoing connections. Both Crieff and Comrie can be reached by bus from Perth.

BEN VORLICH, 3232FT/985M
STUC A'CHROIN, 3199FT/975M

Map: OS Sheets 51 and 57: GR 629189 and
   GR 617175
Translation: hill of the bay; peak of danger
Pronunciation: stook a kroin

Access Point: Ardvorlich, GR 633232
Distance/ascent: 10mls/3800ft; 16km/1158m
Approx Time: 4-6 hours

🚶 Take the private road from Ardvorlich House
south on to the open hillside in Glen Vorlich.
Follow the track to foot of Coire Buidhe and
take SE side of the corrie to reach the NNE
ridge of Ben Vorlich and to the summit. From
the summit follow the line of fence posts down
to the Bealach an Dubh Choirein and take steep
boulder slope and zig-zag path immediately
right (NW) of the obvious buttress. Reach cairn
at top of buttress and head south to summit of
Stuc a'Chroin.
🦌 Ardvorlich Estate. Tel: 01764-685260.

BEN CHONZIE, 3054FT/931M

Map: OS Sheets 51 and 52: GR 774309
Translation: possibly hill of moss
Pronunciation: ben ee hoan; locally honzee
Access Point: Invergeldie, GR 743272
Distance/ascent: 8mls/2200ft; 13km/671m
Approx Time: 3-5 hours

🚶 From Invergeldie in Glen Lednock take the
right of way up the west side of the burn. At a
track junction just beyond a gate take the right
hand track and follow it across the burn and
ENE up the hillside then NE to broad summit
ridge. A fence can then be followed NW then
NE to summit.
🦌 Invergeldie Estate. Tel: 01760-685240.

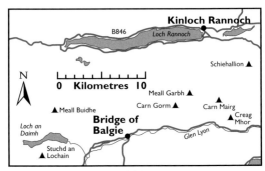

Suggested Base	Aberfeldy
Accommodation	Hotels, guest houses and b/b at Fortingall, Kinloch Rannoch, Kenmore and Aberfeldy. Youth Hostel at Killin. Camping/caravan sites at Kenmore, Kinloch Rannoch, Tummel Bridge and Aberfeldy.
Public Transport	Rail: London, Glasgow and Edinburgh to Inverness. Stations at Perth, Dunkeld and Pitlochry for ongoing buses. Rannoch Station on West Highland Line for ongoing post bus. Buses: Perth and Pitlochry to Aberfeldy, Pitlochry to Kinloch Rannoch. Post Buses: Aberfeldy to Lubreoch in Glen Lyon, Kinloch Rannoch to Rannoch Station.

SCHIEHALLION, 3553FT/1083M

Map: OS Sheet 51: GR 714548
Translation: Fairy Hill of the Caledonians
Pronunciation: shee-hallian
Access Point: Braes of Foss, GR 750559
Distance/ascent: 5mls/2470ft; 8km/753m
Approx Time: 3-5 hours

🐾 Leave the car park and follow the path WSW
across the moorland to join a track coming
from Braes of Foss. This track divides but keep
heading west towards the mountain. The path is
over peaty ground and erosion is severe. Higher
up things improve and the ground is stony.
Continue on east ridge to summit.

🦌 Kynachan Estate. Tel: 01882-632305.

CARN GORM, 3373FT/1028M
MEALL GARBH, 3176FT/968M
CARN MAIRG, 3415FT/1041M
CREAG MHOR, 3218FT/981M

Map: OS Sheet 51: GR 635501, GR 646517, GR
    684513, GR 695496
Translation: blue hill; rough hill; hill of sorrow or
    boundary hill; big rock
Pronunciation: kaarn gorom; myowl garv; kaarn
    mairg; krayk vore
Access Point: Invervar, GR 666483
Distance/ascent: 11mls/4550ft; 18km/1387m
Approx Time: 6-8 hours

🐾 To co-operate with the landowner please walk
this route in a clockwise direction. Follow the
Invervar Burn to the 300-metres contour where
its western tributary should be followed. Follow
steep grassy slopes to summit of Carn Gorm.
Follow broad ridge NNE to An Sgor and the
summit of Meall Garbh. Follow the march fence
to Meall a'Bharr then east and SE over
uninteresting terrain to Carn Mairg. Follow
ridge east of summit to Meall Liath then south
on a wide grassy ridge around the head of
Gleann Muillin to Creag Mhor.

🦌 North Chesthill Estate. Tel: 01887-877207

STUCHD AN LOCHAIN, 3150FT/960M
MEALL BUIDHE, 3058FT/932M

Map: OS Sheet 51: GR 483448 and GR 498499
Translation: peak of the small loch; yellow hill
Pronunciation: stoochk an lochan; myowl boo-ie
Access Point: Loch an Daimh GR 510436
Distance/ascent: 10mls/3500ft; 16km/1067m

Approx Time: 5-8 hours

🐾 Pass the south end of the dam and climb the
   steep grassy hillside south to reach the ridge
   above Coire Ban. Follow fence posts west to
   Creag an Fheadain, then SSW to Sron Chona
   Choirein then west and NW to summit of
   Stuchd an Lochain. Return to the dam. For
   Meall Buidhe cross to the north end of the dam
   and climb due north up easy slopes to Meall
   a'Phuill. Continue west then NNW along the
   broad ridge to the summit.

🦌 Lochs Estate. Tel: 01887-866224.

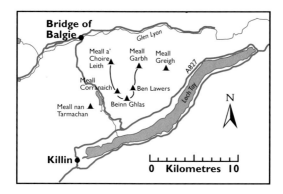

Suggested Base	Killin
Accommodation	Hotels, guest houses and b/b in Killin, Kenmore, Lochearnhead, Fortingall, and Aberfeldy. Youth Hostel at Killin.Camping/caravan sites at Glendochart and Kenmore. Caravan site at Killin.
Public Transport	Rail: Glasgow to Stirling and Perth for ongoing buses. Also Glasgow to Crianlarich with ongoing bus connections. Buses: Stirling to Killin, Perth to Aberfeldy for ongoing post buses. Post Buses: Aberfeldy to Killin and Crianlarich to Killin.

MEALL CORRANAICH, 3507FT/1069M
MEALL A'CHOIRE LEITH, 3038FT/926M

Map: OS Sheet 51: GR 616410, GR 612439
Translation: notched hill or hill of lamenting; hill of the grey corrie
Pronunciation: myowl koraneech; myowl kora lay
Access Point: Summit of Lochan na Lairige Road, GR 594416

Distance/ascent: 8mls/2350ft; 13km/716m
Approx Time: 4-6 hours

🐾 Leave road just north of Lochan and cross
rough moorland SE over peat hags. Reach the
Allt Gleann Da-Eig and follow it uphill to SW
ridge of Meall Corranaich. Leave the summit
and head north down the easy angled ridge.
Keep to the NNE ridge, drop to a col then
follow ridge on the flat topped summit plateau
of Meall a'Choire Leith.

🦌 Roro Estate. Tel: 01887-866216.

BEINN GHLAS, **3619**FT/**1103**M
BEN LAWERS, **3983**FT/**1214**M
MEALL GARBH, **3668**FT/**1118**M
MEALL GREIGH, **3284**FT/**1001**M

Map: OS Sheet 51: GR 626404, GR 636414,
GR 644437, GR 674437
Translation: green/grey hill; possibly loud hill or
hoofed hill; rough hill; hill of the horse studs
Pronunciation: byn glas; byn lors; myowl garv;
myowl gray
Access Point: Lawers on A827, GR 680400
Distance/ascent: 12mls/5750ft; 19km/1753m
Approx Time: 7-10 hours

🐾 Take private road to Machuim Farm. Beyond
the farm follow track east of the Lawers Burn.
Climb due north to Meall Greigh on easy grassy
slopes. Follow west ridge to Meall Garbh. This
ridge is broad and featureless and navigation
can be tricky in misty weather. Follow ridge
around the head of Coire na Cat over the
subsidiary tops of An Stuc and Creag an
Fhithich to steep slopes which lead to Ben
Lawers. From summit follow east ridge down to
Beinn Ghlas then obvious footpath which leads
SW to the National Trust for Scotland centre.
Follow public road back to A827 at
Erdamucky.

🦌 National Trust for Scotland. No restrictions.

Descending the slopes of Ben Lawers towards Beinn Ghlas

MEALL NAN TARMACHAN, 3422FT/1043M

Map: OS Sheet 51: GR 585390
Translation: hill of the ptarmigan
Pronunciation: myowl nan taramachan
Access Point: Bridge over Allt a'Mhoirneas, GR 603382
Distance/ascent: 8mls/2440ft; 13km/744m
Approx Time: 4-6 hours

🐾 Leave the bridge and follow a track beneath a broad ridge. Climb easy grass slopes to a knoll on the 914.4-metres contour. Turn NW and climb various terraces to the summit of Meall nan Tarmachan. It's well worthwhile following the rest of the Tarmachan ridge westwards before leaving Creag na Caillich by its south ridge, then east and back to the track which leads to the starting point.

🦌 National Trust for Scotland. No restrictions.

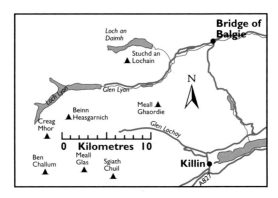

Suggested Base	Killin
Accommodation	Hotels, guest houses, b/b in Killin, Kenmore, Lochearnhead, Fortingall and Aberfeldy. Youth Hostels at Killin and Crianlarich. Camping/caravan sites at Glendochart and Kenmore. Caravan site at Killin.
Public Transport	Rail: Glasgow to Stirling and Perth for ongoing buses. Also Glasgow to Crianlarich with ongoing bus connnection to Killin. Buses: Stirling to Killin, Perth to Aberfeldy for ongoing post buses. Post Buses: Aberfeldy to Killin and Crianlarich to Killin.

MEALL GHAORDIE, 3409FT/1039M

Map: OS Sheet 51: GR 514397
Translation: possibly rounded hill of the shoulder, arm, hand
Pronunciation: myowl girday
Access Point: Tullich in Glen Lochay, GR 516369
Distance/ascent: 4mls/2700ft; 6km/823m

Approx Time: 3-5 hours

🐾 From near the farm of Tullich climb easy
though fairly uninteresting slopes in a north
then NW direction. Pass some small rock
outcrops and reach the summit soon
afterwards. The OS trig point stands inside a
circular cairn.

🦌 Boreland Estate. Tel: 01567-820562

CREAG MHOR, 3438FT/1048M
BEINN HEASGARNICH, 3530FT/1076M

Map: OS Sheets 50 and 51: GR 390361, and GR
413383
Translation: big rock; sheltered hill
Pronunciation: krayk vore; byn heskarneech
Access Point: Badour in Glen Lochay, GR 431351
Distance/ascent: 10 mls/4000ft; 16km/1219m
Approx Time: 5-8 hours

🐾 Leave the cottage of Badour and follow grassy
slopes in a NW direction making for the top of
Stob an Fhir-bhogha. A broad ridge leads north
and over two slight bumps to the summit hump
of Beinn Heasgarnich. Return to Stob an Fhir-
bhogha and take the SW ridge to the boggy
Bealach na Baintighearna. Find the lochan on
the bealach which gives a good line for the steep
but direct ascent to the top of Creag Mhor. A
more westerly approach offers a less steep
ascent but isn't so direct. Descend by the ESE
ridge, the Sron nan Eun to Batavaime in Glen
Lochay, then along the track to Ken Knock and
the start at Badour.

🦌 Ben Challum Estates. Tel: 01567-820278.

BEINN CHALLUM, 3363FT/1025M

Map: OS Sheet 50: GR 387323
Translation: Malcolm's hill
Pronunciation: byn cha-lam
Access Point: Kirkton Farm in Strathfillan,
GR 359284. Leave cars by roadside.
Distance/ascent: 7mls/3000ft; 11km/914m
Approx Time: 4-6 hours

🐾 From the remains of St Fillan's Chapel near the farm follow the track uphill and cross the West Highland railway line. Leave the path and take to the untracked hillside in a NE direction. Continue over grassy slopes, then over some flatter ground and a slight knoll where a fence to your right shows the direction uphill. Where the fence ends walk a few hundred metres to pass a small cairn, then a short distance beyond is the south top at 3270 ft/997m. The summit lies to the north but descend slightly west from the south top for a few metres to find the ridge which descends gradually then gives a steep pull to the large summit cairn.

🦌 Loch Dochart Estate. Tel: 01838-300295.

MEALL GLAS, 3150FT/960M
SGIATH CHUIL, 3067FT/935M

Map: OS Sheets 51: GR 431322 and GR 463318
Translation: grey-green hill; back wing
Pronunciation: *myowl glas; skeea-chool*
Access Point: Lubchurrin in Glen Lochay, GR 453357
Distance/ascent: 8mls/3800ft; 13km/1158m
Approx Time: 4-7 hours

🐾 Follow the stream south of Lubchurrin cottage. Keep east of the stream and follow the broad heather ridge which leads to Meall a'Churain. Follow the obvious level ridge to the summit of Sgiath Chuil. Return almost to Meall a'Churain, and descend the steep, stony slopes west, half a mile to the bealach. Continue west up gradual slopes to the summit of Beinn Cheataich. Follow the ridge SW to a small cairned top then continue along a broad, slightly curved ridge around the rim of Coire Cheathaich. A gentle rise leads to the summit of Meall Glas. Descend the NW ridge to Glen Lochay or take a direct line across Coire Cheathaich back to Lubchurrin.

🦌 Auchlyne Estate. Tel: 01567-820487.

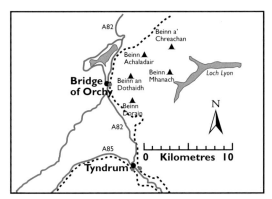

Suggested Base Accommodation	Bridge of Orchy or Tyndrum Hotels, guest houses, b/b at Bridge of Orchy, Inveroran, Kingshouse and Tyndrum, Crianlarich, Glen Coe. Youth Hostels at Crianlarich and Glencoe. Private bunkhouses at Bridge of Orchy and Kingshouse. Camping/caravan site at Glencoe. Caravan site at Tyndrum.
Public Transport	Rail: Bridge of Orchy is on the West Highland Line. London and Glasgow to Fort William. Buses: Glasgow to Fort William for Bridge of Orchy.

BEINN DORAIN, 3530FT/1076M
BEINN AN DOTHAIDH, 3287FT/1002M

Map: OS Sheet 50: GR 326378, GR 332408
Translation: hill of the otter or small stream; hill of the scorching
Pronunciation: *byn doa-ran; byn an daw-ee*
Access Point: Bridge of Orchy Station, GR 301394
Distance/ascent: 8mls/3600ft; 13km/1097m
Approx Time: 5-7 hours

� Leave the railway station and make for the
obvious col on the skyline between the two hills.
At the col climb due south following an obvious
path up an easy angled ridge then along the
edge of a rocky escarpment. Continue up broad
grassy slopes to a bouldery summit. The real
summit lies about 656 feet/200 metres further
south. Return to the col and climb a diagonal
line NNE to the summit of Beinn an Dothaidh.
The highest top is the central one. Return to
the col and descend Coire an Dothaidh to
Bridge of Orchy.

🦌 Auch Estate. Tel: 01838-400233.

BEINN MHANACH, 3130FT/954M

Map: OS Sheet 50: GR 373412
Translation: monk hill
Pronunciation: byn vanach
Access Point: A82 near Auch, GR 317353
Distance/ascent: 12mls/2800ft; 19km/853m
Approx Time: 5-8 hours

🦌 Leave cars by the A82. Walk down the road
past Auch, under the viaduct and up the Auch
Glen track. Continue on the track, which
crosses the burn several times to the watershed
where the long steep grassy slopes lead to Beinn
a'Churin, 3020 feet/920m. A broad and flat
ridge runs east to the summit of Beinn
Mhanach.

🦌 Auch Estate. Tel: 01838-400233.

BEINN ACHALADAIR, 3409FT/1039M
BEINN A'CHREACHAIN, 3547FT/1081M

Map: OS Sheet 50: GR 345434, GR 373441
Translation: field of hard water; hill of the
clamshell
Pronunciation: byn achalatur; byn a chree-achan
Access Point: Achallader Farm car park,
GR 322444
Distance/ascent: 9mls/3900ft; 14km/1189m
Approx Time: 6-8 hours

From the farm head south along a track, over the railway and up Coire Achaladair. Climb to the col at the head of the corrie then turn north along the grassy ridge to the south top of Beinn Achaladair. Continue along the ridge to the summit. Descend east along the corrie rim and descend to the col at 2625 feet/800m. Follow the broad ridge over the flat top of Meall Buidhe and then up the stony slopes of Beinn Chreachain. Descend by the steep NE ridge and once the crags are avoided turn WNW to descend grassy slopes, past the Lochan a'Chreachain, past scattered birches and through the pines of Crannach Wood. Cross the railway by a footbridge and take the track by the Water of Tulla back to the farm.

Black Mount Estate. Tel: 01838-400225.

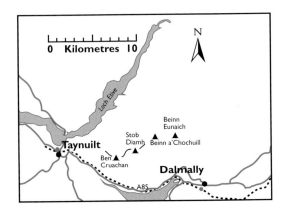

Suggested Base Dalmally
Accommodation Hotels, guest houses, b/b at
Dalmally, Lochawe, Connel and
Oban. Youth Hostel at Oban.
Camping/caravan site at Ledaig,
North Connel.
Public Transport Rail: Glasgow to Oban stopping
at Dalmally, Taynuilt and
Connel. Buses: Glasgow and
Edinburgh to Oban for
Dalmally, Taynuilt and Connel.

BEN CRUACHAN, 3694FT/1126M
STOB DIAMH, 3274FT/998M

Map: OS Sheet 50: GR 069304, GR 095308
Translation: stacky hill; peak of the stag
Pronunciation: byn kroo-achan; stop dyv
Access Point: Falls of Cruachan, GR 078268
Distance/ascent: 9mls/4900ft; 14km/1494m
Approx Time: 5-8 hours

ᴁ Climb steeply up the path beside the Allt
Cruachan to the Cruachan dam access road.
For an east-west round of Cruachan's tops
follow the reservoir's eastern shore before

---

climbing the grassy slopes to Stob Garbh.
Continue north, descend slightly then climb to
the summit of Stob Diamh. Follow the west
ridge over the Drochaid Glas, (which lies
slightly north of the main line of the ridge) then
along a narrower bouldery crest to the main
summit of Cruachan. The ridge continues to a
bealach and the 'Taynuilt Peak', Stob Dearg.
Return to the bealach, re-ascend the main peak
for some distance to avoid the slabby face of
Coire a'Bhachaill, then head due south to Meall
Cuanail and the grassy slopes back to the
Cruachan dam.

🦌 Castles Estate. Tel: 01838-200247.

BEINN A'CHOCUILL, 3215FT/980M
BEINN EUNAICH, 3245FT/989M

Map: OS Sheet 50: GR 110328, GR 136328
Translation: hill of the hood; fowling hill
Pronunciation: byn a cho-chil; byn ayneech
Access Point: Drishaig, GR 133283
Distance/ascent: 8mls/3900ft; 13km/1189m
Approx Time: 5-8 hours

🐾 From the bridge over the Allt Mhoille on the
B8077 road follow the track which runs to the
head of Glen Noe. At the 381 metres contour
another short track bears right. Follow this and
continue up the SE rib of Beinn a'Chocuill to
the summit ridge and the cairn half a mile
further west. Return along the ridge to its east
end where it drops to a high bealach which is
crossed to the shoulder of Beinn Eunaich.
Broad grassy slopes lead back to the start over
the subsidiary top of Stob Maol.

🦌 Castles Estate. Tel: 01838-200247.

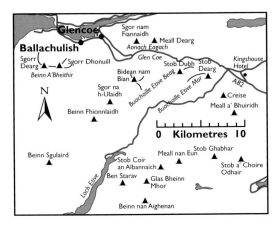

Suggested Base Accommodation	Glencoe or Kingshouse Hotels, guest houses and b/b in Glencoe, Ballachulish and Kingshouse. Youth hostel in Glencoe. Camping/caravan sites in Glencoe and Onich. Private bunkhouses at Clachaig and Leacantium, Glencoe and at Kingshouse Hotel.
Public Transport	Rail: Glasgow to Fort William. Nearest station at Fort William or Bridge of Orchy for connecting buses. Buses: Glasgow to Fort William for Kingshouse, Glencoe and Ballachulish. Oban to Fort William for Ballachulish.

BEN STARAV, 3537FT/1078M
GLAS BHEINN MHOR, 3271FT/997M
BEINN NAN AIGHENAN, 3150FT/960M

Map: OS Sheet 50: GR 126427, GR 153429 and GR 149405

High in the Blackmount Deer Forest

Translation: unknown; big green/grey hill and hill of the hinds
Pronunciation: *byn sta-rav; glas vyn voar; ben yan yanan*
Access Point: Glen Etive, GR 136467
Distance/ascent: 12mls/5600ft; 19km/1707m
Approx Time: 5-8 hours

&#x0; Approach from Glen Etive where a track crosses the river to Coileitir Farm. Follow a moorland path, rough in places to a bridge on the Allt Mheuran and a path on its west bank. After quarter of a mile take the broad lower slopes of the N ridge of Ben Starav. Follow this ridge, which narrows noticeably and becomes quite rocky, to the triangulation pillar near the summit. The summit cairn sits a short distance to the south-east. From the cairn follow the ridge SE and east to the top of Stob Coire Dheirg and then follow another twist in the ridge to where it turns ESE and drops to an obvious bealach west of the grassy slopes of Glas Bheinn Mhor. From this bealach head SSE to the broad ridge leading to Beinn nan Aighenan. From the summit, retrace your steps back to the bealach west of Glas Bheinn Mhor, turn east and cross the grassy subsidiary top and finish up a rockier ridge to the summit. Return to Glen Etive by Glas Bheinn Mhor's east ridge, then north into the corrie at the head of the Allt Mheuran. Glas Bheinn Mhor's

north ridge is steep and can often pose hazards
in snow or when the grass is very wet.

🦌 Glen Kinglass Estate. Tel: 01866-822271.

STOB COIR'AN ALBANNAICH, 3425FT/1044M
MEALL NAN EUN, 3045FT/928M

Map: OS Sheet 50: GR 169433, GR 192449
Translation: peak of the corrie of the Scotsmen;
hill of the birds
*Pronunciation: stop kor an alapaneech; myowl
nan ayn*
Access Point: As for Ben Starav
Distance/ascent: 9mls/4300ft; 14km/1311m
Approx Time: 5-8 hours

🐾 Leave Glen Etive but before reaching Coileitir
Farm head SE uphill through open woodland.
Reach the broad NW shoulder of Stob Coir'an
Albannaich and follow this ridge to the summit.
The continuation to Meall nan Eun involves an
awkward switchback ridge and crosses the
subsidiary summit of Meall Tarsuinn. The route
is obvious in clear conditions but requires
careful navigation when weather is poor. From
the summit of Meall nan Eun go NW across the
plateau and descend in a NW direction towards
the waters of the Allt Ceitlein. There is
eventually a path on its north bank which takes
you back to Glen Etive.

🦌 Glen Kinglass Estate. Tel: 01866-822271.

STOB GHABHAR, 3566FT/1087M
STOB A'CHOIRE ODHAIR, 3094FT/943M

Map: OS Sheet 50: GR 230455, GR 258461
Translation: peak of the goat; peak of the dun-
coloured corrie
Pronunciation: stop gowar; stop a corrie oor
Access Point: Victoria Bridge, GR 271423
Distance/ascent: 12mls/4550ft; 19km/1387m
Approx Time: 5-8 hours

🐾 From Victoria Bridge follow the track which
leads west along the north bank of the Linne
nam Beathach. Reach a small corrugated iron

hut after about 600 metres and take the path which runs north from it beside the Allt Toaig. At GR 252446, the path crosses another burn and west of it a broad ridge lifts up to Beinn Toaig and the broad plateau-like ridge which is crowned by the summit of Stob a'Choire Odhair. Descend west to a wide knolly bealach, continue west uphill for a few hundred yards, then turn SW and up steep slopes to reach a ridge called the Aonach Eagach. Follow this ridge, which is narrow and exposed in places, to where it meets the broad SE ridge of Stob Ghabhar. Follow this to the summit. Return by way of the SE ridge.

🦌 Black Mount Estate. Tel: 01838-400225/400269.

CREISE, 3609FT/1100M
MEALL A'BHUIRIDH, 3635FT/1108M

Map: OS Sheet 41: GR 238507, GR 251503
Translation: unknown; hill of the rutting stags
Pronunciation: *kraysh; myowl a vooree*
Access Point: Blackrock Cottage, GR 268531
Distance/ascent: 8mls/3200ft; 13km/975m
Approx Time: 4-6 hours

🥾 Cross the heather moorland to the mouth of the Cam Ghleann to gain the rocky slopes of Sron na Creise. Contour west to avoid rocky difficulties and ascend steep grass and scree slopes to Stob a'Ghlais Choire, the start of the main ridge which eventually terminates at Stob Ghabhar in the south. Follow the corrie rim round to a curved crest which rises to Creise. Follow the ridge towards the flat top of Mam Coire Easain. An interesting stony rib offers a way of escape from the ridge towards a bealach at the foot of Meall a'Bhuiridh. Take care in poor conditions as navigation can be tricky and cornices can pose problems in winter. Climb to the summit of Meall a' Bhuiridh and then descend back to Blackrock Cottage by way of the ski paraphernalia.

🦌 Black Mount Estate. Tel: 01838-400225/400269.

BEINN SGULAIRD, 3074FT/937M

Map: OS Sheet 50: GR 053461
Translation: unknown
Pronunciation: byn skoolard
Access Point: Elleric, GR 035489
Distance/ascent: 4mls/3050ft; 6km/930m
Approx Time: 3-5 hours

⚐ Leave the small car park at Elleric and take the
   track past the house to a bridge on the River
   Ure near Glenure House. Beyond the house
   take the steeply rising ground SSE as the most
   direct ascent to the summit ridge. Descend
   either by the SW and west ridges to the head of
   Loch Creran, or alternatively NE and east to
   the headwaters of the River Ure, then follow
   the river back to Glenure.
⚐ West Highlands Estates Office, Fort William.
   Tel: 01397-702433.

BEINN FHIONNLAIDH, 3146FT/959M

Map: OS Sheet 41: GR 095498
Translation: Finlay's Hill
Pronunciation: byn yoonly
Access Point: Elleric, GR 035489
Distance/ascent: 9mls/3140ft; 14km/957m
Approx Time: 5-7 hours

⚐ Start at Glenure, (see access for Beinn
   Sgulaird), and take the lower grassy slopes in a
   NE direction towards Leac Bharainn. Above
   this the obvious west ridge rises gradually to the
   summit of Beinn Fhionnlaidh. Descend the
   same way. An ascent from Glen Etive, once the
   popular route to the summit, cannot now be
   recommended because of Forestry Commission
   activities.
⚐ West Highland Estates Office, Fort William.
   Tel: 01397-702433.

SGOR NA H-ULAIDH, 3261FT/994M

Map: OS Sheet 41: GR 111518
Translation: peak of the treasure

Pronunciation: skor na hoolya
Access Point: Achnacon, GR 118565
Distance/ascent: 8mls/3600ft; 13km/109m
Approx Time: 4-6 hours

🐾 Follow the landrover track which follows the west bank of the Allt na Muidhe. Not far before the cottage of Gleann-leac-na-muidhe leave the track and take to the steep prow of Aonach Dubh a'Ghlinne, a fierce ascent which threads through several rocky outcrops. Continue south on the ridge to the top of Stob an Fhuarain. Descend SW to the bealach and follow the remains of an ancient wall and fence along the crest of the ridge up increasingly rocky ground to the summit. From the summit continue west to the spur of Corr na Beinne and carefully descend its steep north slopes to a col. From here easy slopes to the NE take you to the headwaters of the Allt na Muidhe.

🦌 Forestry Commission. Tel: 01631-566155.

BUACHAILLE ETIVE MOR, STOB DEARG, 3353FT/1022M

Map: OS Sheet 41: GR 223543
Translation: big herdsman of Etive, red peak
Pronunciation: booachil etiv moar; stop jerrack
Access Point: Altnafeath, GR 221563
Distance/ascent: 5mls/2600ft; 8km/792m
Approx Time: 3-5 hours

🐾 Follow the track to the bridge over the River Coupall and pass the white climbers' hut called Lagangarbh. Take the right fork in the path and continue into Coire na Tulaich following the path on the west bank of the obvious burn. Follow the path up the corrie to its head where scree slopes offer difficult access to a flat bealach. Turn east and cross red and pink boulders and scree heading east then NE along a ridge which narrows appreciably towards the summit. The complete traverse of the Buachaille Etive Mor ridge is a rewarding walk, from Stob Dearg to Stob na Broige, returning to Altnafeath by the Lairig Gartain pass to the NNW.

🦌 National Trust for Scotland. No restrictions.

BUACHAILLE ETIVE BEAG, STOB DUBH, 3143FT/958M

Map: OS Sheet 41: GR 179535
Translation: small herdsman of Etive, black peak
Pronunciation: booachil etiv baik, stop doo
Access Point: A82 road, GR 188563
Distance/ascent: 5mls/2400ft; 8km/732m
Approx Time: 3-5 hours

🚶 Follow the signpost which indicates the right of way from 'Lairig Eilde to Glen Etive'. Take the path for about quarter of a mile before leaving it for the open hillside in a southerly direction. Head for the bealach to the NE of Stob Coire Raineach, and then climb this top. Follow the obvious ridge onwards to Stob Dubh at the end of the Buachaille Etive Beag ridge. An alternative route climbs Stob Dubh from Dalness in Glen Etive and takes the hill's SSW ridge.

🦌 National Trust for Scotland. No restrictions.

BIDEAN NAM BIAN, 3773FT/1150M

Map: OS Sheet 41: GR 143542
Translation: peak of the mountains
Pronunciation: beetyan nam beeoan
Access Point: Achnambeithach, west of Loch Achtriochtan, GR 139567
Distance/ascent: 5mls/3250ft; 8km/991m
Approx Time: 4-7 hours

🚶 Follow the path which climbs up into Coire nam Beith on the west side of the stream. Pass some very fine waterfalls and climb high into the corrie. At a confluence of streams just above the 500-metres contour line take a SSW direction up steep slopes of grass and scree to reach the main ridge of the mountain just WNW of Stob Coire nam Beith. Follow the obvious path on the ridge to the summit, then SE to the west peak of Bidean nam Bian and then east to the summit. As an alternative descent route follow the ridge SE and return to

the A82 by the Coire Gabhail or Lairig Eilde.
Another alternative is to link Stob Coire nan
Lochan and then descend Coire nan Lochan to
the A82.

Staking Information: National Trust for Scotland.
No restrictions.

AONACH EAGACH RIDGE, MEALL DEARG, 3127FT/953M
SGOR NAM FIANNAIDH, 3173FT/967M

Map: OS Sheet 41: GR 161584, GR 141583
Translation: notched ridge, red hill; peak of the
   fair haired warriors
Pronunciation: *myowl d-yerrack; skoor nam
   feeanee*
Access Point: Allt-na-reigh, GR 176566
Distance/ascent: 4 mls/3000ft; 6km/914m
Approx Time: 3-5 hours

Follow the path behind the house of Allt-na-
reigh up the grassy slopes of Am Bodach. There
are a few rocky outcrops but these can be
avoided on the east. To reach the crest of the
Aonach Eagach ridge follow the edge of the
crags to the left of Am Bodach's cairn in a
WNW direction. A sudden drop with a 20-
metre scramble on good but polished holds
starts the ridge traverse proper. Follow the
crest of the ridge to the grassy hump of Meall
Dearg. From Meall Dearg follow the line of
fence posts along the crest and then traverse
the Crazy Pinnacles. This involves some
exposed scrambling on the most sensational
section of the ridge. After the Pinnacles more
fence posts accompany you on the long pull to
Stob Coire Leith, before the ridge levels out
towards the second Munro, Sgor nam
Fiannaidh. It is advised to descend due south of
this summit, picking a route with care through
rocky outcrops and grassy slopes. The
alternative descent is half a mile further west of
the summit and follows a very eroded path on
the west side of Clachaig Gully. This path has a
lot of loose stones and rock on it and there is a
danger of knocking scree into the gully where
climbers could well be put in danger. There is

also the danger of actually falling into the gully. There have been several fatalities at this point in recent years.

🦌 National Trust for Scotland. No restrictions.

BEINN A'BHEITHIR, SGORR DHEARG, 3360FT/1024M
SGORR DHONUILL, 3284FT/1001M

Map: OS Sheet 41: GR 056558, GR 040555
Translation: hill of the thunderbolt, red peak; Donald's peak
Pronunciation: *byn vair, skoor d-yerrack; skoor ghawil*
Access Point: A828, GR 044595
Distance/ascent: 10mls/400ft; 16km/1219m
Approx Time: 5-8 hours

🥾 Leave the road about 800 metres west of the Ballachulish Bridge on a minor road which leads you to some houses at the foot of Gleann a'Chaolais. Cars can be left here. Follow a Forestry Commission road south and after a while it zig-zags up steeper ground, passes an old quarry and comes to a crossroads. Go straight across, round another bend, over a bridge and cross a burn at GR 047569. A cairn by the track indicates the path which climbs SE through the forest and on to the open hillside above the trees. Climb south to the obvious bealach between to the two peaks of Beinn a'Bheither, Sgorr Dhonuill on your right and Sgorr Dhearg on your left. Both peaks are easily reached from the bealach.

🦌 Forestry Commission. Tel: 01631-566155.

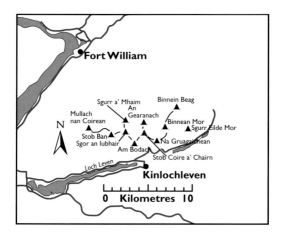

Suggested Base	Fort William
Accommodation	Hotels, guest houses and b/b at Fort William, Kinlochleven, Onich, Spean Bridge, Roybridge. Youth Hostel at Glen Nevis. Private Hostels at Achriabach, Glen Nevis and Roybridge. Camping/caravan sites at Glen Nevis, Roybridge and Spean Bridge.
Public Transport	Rail: Glasgow to Fort William. Stations at Tulloch, Roybridge and Spean Bridge. Buses: Glasgow to Skye for Kinlochleven, Fort William and Spean Bridge. Edinburgh to Skye for Fort William; to Aviemore for Tulloch, Roybridge and Spean Bridge. Fort William to Glen Nevis, Fort William to Kinlochleven.

BINNEIN BEAG, 3084FT/940M
BINNEIN MOR, 3701FT/1128M
NA GRUAGAICHEAN, 3461FT/1055M
SGURR EILDE MOR, 3307FT/1008M

Map: OS Sheet 41: GR 222677, GR 212663,
   GR 203652, GR 231658
Translation: small peak; big peak; the maidens;
   big peak of the hind
Pronunciation: beenyan beck; beenyan mor; na
   grooakeechan; skoor ailta moar
Access Point: Glen Nevis Polldubh car park,
   GR 169692
Distance/ascent: 16mls/4500ft; 26km/1372m
Approx Time: 7-10 hours

🏃 Leave the car park at the head of Glen Nevis
   and follow the track through to Steall and along
   the north bank of the Water of Nevis to GR
   215690. Cross the river here and climb the NE
   slopes of Binnein Beag. From the summit head
   SSW, past a lochan and climb the narrow and
   interesting NE ridge of Binnein Mor. Continue
   south on a narrow ridge from the summit to a
   subsidiary top and then SW to the twin summits
   of Na Gruagaichean. The first summit reached,
   the SE summit, is the highest. Retrace your
   steps to the subsidiary top south of Binnein
   Mor and continue on a narrowing ridge to the
   SE to Coire an Lochain. Climb the SW slopes of
   Sgurr Eilde Mor over fairly unpleasant scree
   and boulder fields. Descend by NE ridge to
   Tom an Eite, and return to Glen Nevis by the
   Water of Nevis path.
🦌 West Highlands Estates Office, Fort William.
   Tel: 01397-702433.

AN GEARANACH, 3222FT/982M
STOB CHOIRE A'CHAIRN, 3218FT/981M
AM BODACH, 3386FT/1032M
SGOR AN IUBHAIR, 3286FT/1001M
SGURR A'MHAIM, 3606FT/1099M

Map: OS Sheet 41: GR 188670, GR 185661,
   GR 176651, GR 165655, GR 165667
Translation: the complainer; peak of the corrie of

Sgurr a'Mhaim

the cairn; the old man; peak of the yew; peak of
the large rounded hill

Pronunciation: *an gyeranach; stob corrie a cairn;
am podach; skoor an yooar; skoor a vaim*

Access Point: Glen Nevis Polldubh car park,
GR 169692

Distance/ascent: 9mls/4000ft; 8km/1219m

Approx Time: 4-7 hours

As per route for previous entry, but cross the
Water of Nevis by the wire bridge at the Steall
climbing hut. Go east past the hut, past the
waterfall and a wooded buttress until the path
turns south up a small glen. Continue on the
path which eventually takes long zig-zags and in
time takes you on to the NNE spur of An
Gearanach (unmarked on the OS map).
Continue south from the summit along the short
ridge to An Garbhanach. From this top
continue SW for a short distance and climb to
the summit of Stob Choire a'Chairn. From here
the obvious ridge links SW to Am Bodach, then
WNW to Sgor an Iubhair. North of Sgor an
Iubhair, the Devil's Ridge links with Stob
Choire a'Mhail. While this ridge is narrow with
steep drops on either side it poses no real
problem in good conditions. From here the
slopes open on to the wide quartzy summit
slopes of Sgurr a'Mhaim and then a long
descent northwards to Glen Nevis.

West Highland Estates Office, Fort William.
Tel: 01397-702433.

STOB BAN, 3277FT/999M
MULLACH NAN COIREAN, 3081FT/939M

Map: OS Sheet 41: GR 148654, GR 122662
Translation: light-coloured peak; summit of the
    corries
Pronunciation: stop baan; mullach nan kooran
Access Point: Achriabhach in Glen Nevis, GR
    143685
Distance/ascent: 9mls/4000ft; 14km/1219m
Approx Time: 4-7 hours

🦶 Go through the gate opposite the cottages at
Achriabhach and take the footpath through the
trees (not the forestry road). After a climb the
footpath converges on the forestry road. Turn
the next bend on the east side of the stream and
go out of the forest. Reach the NNE ridge of
Mullach and follow this to the summit. Descend
easy slopes to the SE and follow an undulating
ridge which goes SE then south to the Mullach's
SE top. Soon the ridge drops east to the col
between the two mountains. Climb east then
south up angular boulders and screes to the
summit of Stob Ban. To descend take the
shattered east ridge of Stob Ban to reach a
stalkers' path at the head of Coire a'Mhusgain.
Follow the path north down the corrie back to
Achriabhach.

🦶 West Highland Estates Office, Fort William.
Tel: 01397-702433.

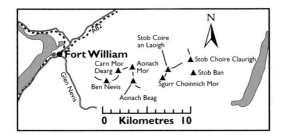

Suggested Base	Fort William
Accommodation	Hotels, guest houses and b/b at Fort William, Spean Bridge, Roybridge. Youth Hostels at Glen Nevis and Loch Lochy. Private Hostel at Achriabhach, Glen Nevis. Camping/caravan sites at Glen Nevis, Roybridge and Spean Bridge.
Public Transport	Rail: Glasgow to Fort William. Stations at Tulloch, Roybridge and Spean Bridge. Buses: Glasgow to Skye for Kinlochleven, Fort William and Spean Bridge. Edinburgh to Skye for Fort William; to Aviemore for Tulloch, Roybridge and Spean Bridge. Fort William to Glen Nevis. Fort William to Kinlocheven.

BEN NEVIS, 4409FT/1344M
CARN MOR DEARG, 4012FT/1223M

Map: OS Sheet 41: GR 166713, GR 177722
Translation: possibly venomous mountain; big red hill
Pronunciation: byn nevis; caarn more jerrack
Access Point: Achintee, GR 125731
Distance/ascent: 13mls/5800ft; 21km/1769m
Approx Time: 7-10 hours

Ben Nevis from Carn Mor Dearg

🏃 Leave Achintee and follow the obvious Ben
Nevis track as far as Lochan Meall at t-Suidhe.
The track to Ben Nevis continues on a series of
broad zig-zags above but to reach Carn Mor
Dearg continue past the loch around the flanks
of Carn Dearg to drop down into the valley of
the Allt a'Mhuilinn. Cross the river near point
GR 154739 and climb east up rough bouldery
slopes to Carn Beag Dearg. Continue SSE on
ridge over Carn Dearg Meadhonach to Carn
Mor Dearg. To continue to Ben Nevis follow the
ridge south and cross the Carn Mor Dearg
arête. Where the arête abuts on to the bulk of
Ben Nevis, climb west over blocks and boulders
to the summit. Take care in this area in
conditions of snow cover. Many walkers have
slipped from this point into Coire Leis below.
🦌 West Highland Estates Office, Fort William.
Tel: 01397-702433.

AONACH BEAG, 4048FT/1234M
AONACH MOR, 4006FT/1221M

Map: OS Sheet 41: GR 196715, GR 193730
Translation: little ridge; big (broad) ridge
Pronunciation: oenach bayk; oenach more
Access Point: Polldubh car park, Glen Nevis
    GR 167691
Distance/ascent: 14mls/4880ft; 22km/1488m
Approx Time: 7-10 hours

☆ Take the footpath which runs through the Nevis
Gorge to Steall. Pass the wire bridge and
continue to the bridge and ruin by the Allt
Coire Giubhsachan. Follow the stream north to
the obvious bealach east of Carn Mor Dearg.
Climb a steep slope east to the bealach between
Aonach Mor and Aonach Beag. From the
bealach continue north for one kilometre over a
broad and featureless ridge to the summit of
Aonach Mor. Return the way you came to the
bealach below Aonach Beag and climb rocky
slopes SE to the summit. Descend to the Allt
Coire Giubhsachan by the SW ridge and return
to Steall.

☙ West Highland Estates Office, Fort William.
Tel: 01397-702433.

SGURR CHOINNICH MOR, 3592FT/1095M
STOB COIRE AN LAOIGH, 3658FT/1115M
STOB CHOIRE CLAURIGH, 3861FT/1177M
STOB BAN, 3205FT/977M

Map: OS Sheet 41: GR 227714, GR 240725,
GR 262739, GR 266724
Translation: big peak of the moss; peak of the
corrie of the calf; peak of the corrie of
clamouring; light coloured peak
Pronunciation: skoor choanyeech more; stop
corrie an looee; stop corrie clowree; stop baan
Access Point: Coirechoille, GR 252807
Distance/ascent: 20mls/6600ft; 32km/2012m
Approx Time: 10-12 hours

☆ Take the land rover track past Coirechoille
farm and through the forest to the Lairig
Leacach. Follow the track to the hut beside the
Allta'Chuil Choirean. Just beyond this strike
uphill in a SW direction up the ENE ridge of
Stob Ban. Follow this ridge to the summit. Take
care on the descent to the bealach between Stob
Ban and Stob Coire Claurigh as the north
slopes are precipitous and very loose. Descend
slightly to the west. Above the bealach, and its
small lochan, there is a sharp pull up to
Claurigh on loose scree and blocks. From the
summit follow the broad crest west to Stob

Aonach Beag

a'Choire Leith and Stob Coire Cath na Sine, where the ridge narrows considerably, over Caisteal to Stob Coire an Laoigh. The next top on the ridge is Stob Coire Easain, the north ridge of which takes you back to Coirechoille, but first continue on the Grey Corries ridge to Sgurr Choinnich Mor. Unfortunately there is a big drop in height and you have to retrace your steps back to Stob Coire Easain, thereby doubling the ascent. Follow the north ridge of Stob Coire Easain over Beinn na Sachaich and back to Coirechoille.

🦌 West Highland Estates Office, Fort William. Tel: 01397-702433.

STOB A'CHOIRE MHEADHOIN, 3629FT/1106M
STOB COIRE EASAIN, 3661FT/1116M

Map: OS Sheet 41: GR 316736, GR 308730
Translation: peak of the middle corrie; peak of the corrie of the little waterfall
Pronunciation: stop a kora vane; stop kora esan
Access Point: Fersit, GR 350782
Distance/ascent: 9mls/3300ft; 14km/1006m
Approx Time: 4-6 hours

🚶 From Fersit follow the track to the dam at the north end of Loch Treig below the slopes of Meall Cian Dearg. Climb steep heather slopes in a SW direction to the 760-metres contour and the open ridge. After two small rises in the

ridge continue SSW to the stony summit of Stob
a'Choire Mheadhoin. Descend SW down rocky
slopes to the bealach and ascend a rocky ridge
WSW to Stob Coire Easain. From the summit
follow the NW ridge and drop to the open
moors of Coire Laire where a footpath takes
you back to the British Aluminium Company
railway line and a pleasant track back to
Fersit.

West Highland Estates Office, Fort William.
Tel: 01397-702433.

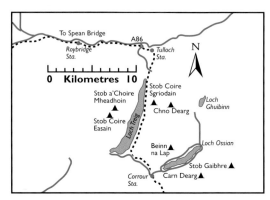

Suggested Base	Roybridge
Accommodation	Private hostels at Roybridge and Newtonmore. Hotels, guest houses and b/b at Spean Bridge and Roybridge
Public Transport	Rail: West Highland Line Glasgow to Fort William stopping at Corrour, Tulloch and Roybridge. Buses: Fort William to Aviemore stopping at Tulloch.

Stob Coire Sgriodain, 3202ft/976m
Chno Dearg, 3435ft/1047m

Map: OS Sheet 41: GR 356744, GR 377741
Translation: peak of the scree corrie; red nut or red hill
Pronunciation: *stop kora sgreeadan; knaw jerrack*
Access Point: Fersit, GR 350782
Distance/ascent: 8mls/3000ft; 13km/914m
Approx Time: 3-5 hours

🚶 From Fersit follow a forestry road east for about 500 metres then take rough ground to the south. Climb open slopes then a craggier ridge

---

to Sron na Garbh-Bheinne. The ridge now narrows and rises to the summit of Stob Coire Sgriodain. Descend south to bealach and then SE to south top of Sgriodain. Cross bumps and knolls in an ESE direction, over a double top and down to another bealach with scattered lochans. Climb easily to the crest of Meall Garbh. Follow ridge NE to the big hump of Chno Dearg. Descend easily NNW to the Strath Ossian to Fersit track.

🦌 Forestry Commission. Enquire at Fersit.

BEINN NA LAP, 3074FT/937M

Map: OS Sheet 41: GR 376676
Translation: possibly mottled hill
Pronunciation: byn na lap
Access Point: Corrour Halt on the West Highland Railway, GR 356664
Distance/ascent: 5mls/1750ft; 8km/533m
Approx Time: 2-4 hours

🚶 Take the train to Corrour Halt on the West Highland Line. Unless you are staying in the vicinity you will have to time your climb to suit the train timetables so check on your return train time. Follow the track east from the station to Loch Ossian. Take the left fork of the track where it splits at the loch and follow it along the north shore of the loch. Leave the track and climb north on easy angled slopes. Reach a broad ridge and follow it ENE to the summit.

🦌 Forestry Commission. Enquire at Fersit.

SGOR GAIBHRE, 3133FT/955M
CARN DEARG, 3087FT/941M

Map: OS Sheets 41 and 42: GR 444674, GR 418661
Translation: goat's peak; red hill
Pronunciation: skor gyra; kaarn jerrack
Access Point: Corrour Halt, GR 356664
Distance/ascent: 12mls/3000ft; 19km/914m
Approx Time: 6-9 hours

🏃 Go ENE from the station along the south shore of Loch Ossian to the cottages at the end of the loch. Avoid the forest on the south side of the loch by crossing the bridge over the outflow of the loch near Corrour Lodge and taking the path NE beside the Uisge Labhair for a short distance. Once clear of the trees cross the open hillside south to gain the slopes of Meall Nathrach Mor. Descend slightly then climb to Sgor Choinnich. Descend south to an obvious bealach and climb the broad but steeper ridge to Sgor Gaibhre. Turn WSW, descend easy slopes to broad bealach called the Mam Ban. Continue in the same direction to Carn Dearg. Descend WNW to the 'Road to the Isles' path and Corrour Station.

🦌 Forestry Commission. Enquire at Fersit.

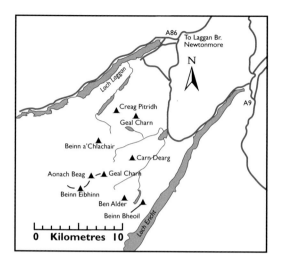

Suggested Base	Laggan
Accommodation	Hotels, b/b at Laggan. Hotels, guest houses and b/b at Dalwhinnie, Newtonmore. Youth Hostel at Loch Ossian. Private Bunkhouse in Newtonmore. Caravan site at Glen Truim near Newtonmore. Camping/caravan site at Newtonmore.
Public Transport	Rail: London, Glasgow and Edinburgh to Inverness. Stations at Pitlochry, Dalwhinnie and Newtonmore. Post Buses: Newtonmore to Kinloch Laggan for Laggan.

CARN DEARG, 3392FT/1034M
GEAL CHARN, 3714FT/1132M
AONACH BEAG, 3655FT/1114M
BEINN EIBHINN, 3609FT/1100M

Map: OS Sheets 41 and 42: GR 504764,
GR 471745, GR 458742, GR 449733
Translation: red hil; white hill; small ridge;
delightful hill
Pronunciation: *kaarn jerrac; gyal chaarn;
oenach byek; byn ayveen*
Access Point: Culra Bothy, GR 355664
Distance/ascent: 14mls/4500ft; 22km/1372m
Approx Time: 6-10 hours

🐾 These are remote mountains and using Culra
Bothy, ten miles (16km) from Dalwhinnie, as an
access point is the best of many choices. From
Culra Bothy climb west and NW on the southern
flanks of Carn Dearg to the summit. Another
cairn, slightly south, leads to the ridge which
drops to a flat bealach and then rises to Diollaid
a'Chairn. Beyond here the ridge narrows and
leads to a steep and terraced buttress-like slope
with fronts the plateau of Geal Charn. Pick a
route through the terraces to the plateau. You
may experience some difficulty locating the
summit cairn, even in clear weather. Beyond the
cairn a long slope leads WSW to a grassy bealach.
Descend to the bealach and climb a short sharp
rise to Aonach Beag. At the cairn, turn sharply
SW to descend down rough terraces to a narrow
bealach above Lochan a'Charra Mhoir. The
ascent of Beinn Eibhinn involves a steep pull to
the curve of a broad ridge, which in turn rises to
the cairn. To return to Culra descend south and
east to the Bealach Dubh path and follow it
through the Bealach back to the bothy.
🦌 Ben Alder Estate. Tel: 01528-522224.

BEN ALDER, 3766FT/1148M
BEINN BHEOIL, 3343FT/1019M

Map: OS Sheet 42: GR 496718, GR 517717
Translation: hill of the rock water; hill of the
mouth

Pronunciation: byn awlder; byn vyawl
Access Point: Ben Alder Cottage, GR 499680.
Walk-in to Ben Alder Cottage from Rannoch
Mill (GR 506576) is 8 miles (12.8km)
Distance/ascent: 8mls/3500ft; 13km/1067m
Approx Time: 4-6 hours

    Follow the path on the east bank of the stream
behind the cottage to the Bealach Breabag. Just
short of the summit of the bealach climb the
broken and craggy slopes west to a ridge high
above the Garbh Coire of Ben Alder. After half
a mile cross the expansive plateau to a high
level lochan and the summit cairn. Return to
the Bealach Breabag and climb the short and
easy slope to Sron Coire na h-Iolaire. This is a
short spur with cairns at either end. To the
north of the west cairn a ridge drops to a stony
bealach which then rises to the slabby summit
slopes of Beinn Bheoil.

    Ben Alder Estate. Tel: 01528-522224.

BEINN A'CHLACHAIR, 3569FT/1088M
GEAL CHARN, 3442FT/1049M
CREAG PITRIDH, 3031FT/924M

Map: OS Sheet 42: GR 471781, GR 504812,
GR 488814
Translation: stonemason's hill; white hill; possibly
Petrie's hill
*Pronunciation: byn a clachar; geel harn; krayk
peetrie*
Access Point: Luiblea, GR 432830
Distance/ascent: 15mls/4000ft; 24km/1219m
Approx Time: 7-9 hours

    Leave the A86 Laggan to Spean Bridge road at
the concrete bridge and follow the bulldozed
road up the east side of the Amhainn Ghuilbinn
for about one kilometre. Turn left and follow
another track for 500 metres, then right along
another track which carries you around the
lower slopes of Binnein Shuas to the head of
Lochan na h-Earba. From the SW corner of the
loch take a stalkers' path which runs up the
hillside beside the Allt Coire Pitridh. After a

distance of about 1.5km bear south on open hillside towards the NE flank of Beinn a'Chlachair. Follow the slops to an obvious shoulder and a rocky ridge around the corrie rim to the summit. Return ENE along a broad ridge which stops above a large crag. Descend north to a stalkers' path with another path a few metres lower. Follow this second path on to the west flank of Geal Charn. Go east and climb easy slopes to the flat summit. Return to the bealach west of Geal Charn and climb the easy slopes to Craig Pitridh. From the summit descend SW to regain the stalkers' path alongside the Allt Coire Pitridh.

🦌 Ardverikie Estate. Tel: 01528-544300.

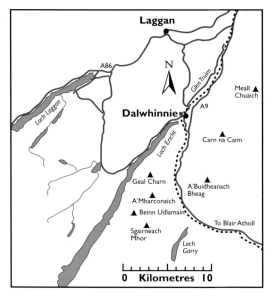

Suggested Base Accommodation	Blair Atholl Hotels, guest houses, b/b. Youth hostel at Pitlochry. Camping/caravan sites at Blair Atholl and Glen Truim, Newtonmore.
Public Transport	Rail: Glasgow and Edinburgh to Inverness, stopping at Pitlochry, Blair Atholl, Dalwhinnie and Kingussie. Buses: London, Glasgow and Edinburgh to Perth and Inverness for Blair Atholl, Dalwhinnie, Newtonmore and Kingussie.

Geal Charn, 3008ft/917m
A'Mharconaich, 3199ft/975m
Beinn Udlamain, 3314ft/1010m
Sgairneach Mhor, 3251ft/991m

Map: OS Sheet 42: GR 597783, GR 604764,
   GR 579740, GR 599732
Translation: white hill; the horse place; gloomy
   mountain; big stony hillside
Pronunciation: *gyal chaarn; a varkaneech; byn
   ootlaman; skaarnyatch vore*
Access Point: Balsporran Cottages, GR 628792
Distance/ascent: 15mls/3750ft; 24km/1143m
Approx Time: 6-10 hours

From the cottages cross the railway and take the
track which runs up Coire Fhar for a short
distance before taking to the open hillside of the
NE ridge of Geal Charn. Pass the three cairns
higher up the ridge at 2750 feet/838 metres then
continue 800 metres west to the summit. Continue
south on a broad whalebacked ridge to a height of
3174 feet where a ridge appears to run off NE.
The summit of A'Mharconaich lies 800 metres
along this ridge. Return to the 3174-feet point
from the summit and cross a wide bealach to the
SW and continue SW on a broad ridge to an
unnamed top at 3213 feet, then over a broad
featureless plateau to the summit of Beinn
Udlamain. To reach Sgairneach Mhor descend
south to a boggy bealach. On the far side take an
easterly bearing to locate the summit cairn on the
most westerly top of the hill. From the summit
descend to Coire Dhomhain via the easterly spur,
then follow the track to the railway and the A9
about 4km south of Balsporran.

North Drumochter Estate. Tel: 01528-522209.

Map: OS Sheet 42: GR 716879
Translation: hill of the quaich
Pronunciation: *myowl chooeech*
Access Point: Cuaich, GR 654876
Distance/ascent: 7mls/2000ft; 11km/610m
Approx Time: 3-5 hours

🐾 Leave the A9 just south of the Cuaich cottages and follow a private road through a locked gate. In a short distance reach a track beside an aqueduct and follow it to the Loch Cuaich dam. The hill is then climbed on open heather slopes to the summit.

🦌 Cuaich Estate. Tel: 01528 522254.

CARN NA CAIM, 3087FT/941M
A'BHUIDHEANACH BHEAG, 3071FT/936M

Map: OS Sheet 42: GR 677822, GR 661776
Translation: cairn of the curve; the little yellow place
Pronunciation: kaarn a kym; a vooanach vek
Access Point: Balsporran Cottages, GR 629792
Distance/ascent: 8mls/2000ft; 13km/610m
Approx Time: 4-6 hours

🐾 Leave the A9 just south of Balsporran and climb steep heathery slopes raked with shallow gullies to Meall a'Chaoruinn. Continue east and follow a fence to the summit of A'Bhuidheanach Bheag. North of the summit the fence crosses an area of peat at the head of Coire Chuirn. Follow the fence to Carn a' Caim, two rounded tops on either side of a shallow depression. Follow open and obvious slopes SW back to the A9 in Drumochter Pass.

🦌 South Drumochter Estate. Tel: 01528-522209.

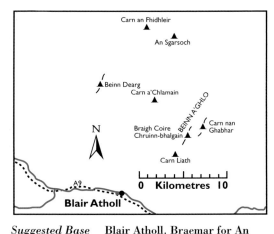

Carn an Fhidhleir

An Sgarsoch

Beinn Dearg
Carn a'Chlamain

BEINN A'GHLO

Braigh Coire
Chruinn-bhalgain

Carn nan
Ghabhar

N

Carn Liath

A9

0   Kilometres   10

Blair Atholl

Suggested Base	Blair Atholl. Braemar for An Sgarsoch and Carn an Fhidhleir.
Accommodation	Hotels, guest houses, b/b. Youth hostels at Pitlochry and Braemar. Camping/caravan sites at Blair Atholl and Braemar.
Public Transport	Rail: Glasgow and Edinburgh to Inverness, stopping at Blair Atholl. Glasgow, Edinburgh and Inverness to Aberdeen. Ongoing bus services to Braemar. Buses: Glasgow and Edinburgh to Inverness, stopping at Blair Atholl. Glasgow, Edinburgh and Inverness to Aberdeen. Aberdeen to Braemar.

BEINN A'GHLO: CARN LIATH, 3199FT/975M
BRAIGH COIRE CHRUINN-BHALGAIN, 3510FT/1070M
CARN NAN GABHAR, 3704FT/1129M

Map: OS Sheet 43: GR 936698, GR 946724,
GR 971733
Translation: grey hill; upland of the corrie of
round blisters; hill of the goats.

Pronunciation: *kaarn leea; bray corrie kroon valaka; kaarn nan gower*
Access Point: Marble Lodge, GR 898717
Distance/ascent: 12mls/4000ft; 19km/1219m
Approx Time: 6-8 hours

Permission is given (on small payment) by Atholl Estate at the factor's office at Old Blair to drive up Glen Tilt as far as Forest Lodge. Behind Balaneasie Cottage on the south bank of the River Tilt, climb grassy slopes to the headwaters of the Fender Burn. Traverse the hillside SE, past the pines beside Craig-choinnich Lodge and then east up steep heather-covered slopes to the summit of Carn Liath. Follow a twisting ridge north. This soon broadens out as it approaches Braigh Coire Chruinn-bhalgain. Continue NE along the ridge for one kilometre before dropping down grassy slopes to cross the Bealach na Fhiodha. Continue east to the slopes which lead to another bealach between Airgiod Bheinn and Carnnan Gabhar and finally NE along a broad and easy ridge to the twin cairns of Carn nan Gabhar. Descend back to Glen Tilt by the north ridge to the bridge below Allt Fheannach.

Tel: 01796-481355.

BEINN DEARG, 3307FT/1008M

Map: OS Sheet 43: GR 853778
Translation: red hill
Pronunciation: *byn jerrack*
Access Point: Old Blair, GR 867667
Distance/ascent: 15mls/2750ft; 24km/838m
Approx Time: 6-8 hours

From Old Blair walk up the private road in Glen Banvie and continue up east side of the Allt an-Seapail to a bothy beside the Allt Sheicheachan. A track continues along the NW side of this stream to the 800-metres contour. From there follow the broad and easy ridge north to the summit.

Tel: 01796-481355.

CARN A'CHLAMAIN, 3159FT/963M

Map: OS Sheet 43: GR 916758
Translation: hill of the kite or buzzard
Pronunciation: kaarn a klaavan
Access Point: Glen Tilt, GR 908720
Distance/ascent: 6mls/2400ft; 10km/732m
Approx Time: 3-4 hours

🐾 A couple of miles south of Forest Lodge in Glen
Tilt a long ridge runs down from the summit of
Carn a'Chlamain just east of the Allt
Craoinidh. Climb steep initial slopes then follow
the curving ridge to the summit.

🦌 Tel: 01796-481355.

AN SGARSOCH, 3300FT/1006M
CARN AN FHIDHLEIR, 3261FT/994M

Map: OS Sheet 43: GR 933836, GR 905842
Translation: the place of sharp rocks; hill of the
fiddler
Pronunciation: an skarsoch; kaarn an yeelar
Access Point: Linn o'Dee, GR 061897
Distance/ascent: 25mls/3000ft; 40km/914m
Approx Time: 10-12 hours

🐾 Follow north bank of the River Dee to White
Bridge and then along the Geldie Burn to
Geldie Lodge. (A mountain bike can be used to
good effect here.) Follow a bulldozed track
WSW to its highest point. Continue SW over
peat hags and climb the NE slopes of Carn an
Fhidhleir to reach the north ridge close to the
summit. Drop SSE along a broad ridge and
then down the east side of the ridge to reach the
bealach at 2297ft/700m. From there climb NE
to the flat summit of An Sgarsoch. Return to
Geldie Lodge by following the north ridge and
then west of Sgarsoch Bheag over peaty ground
to reach the bulldozed track again.

🦌 National Trust for Scotland. No restrictions.

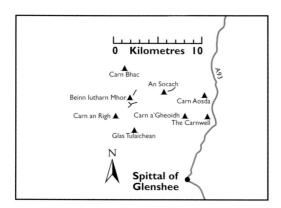

Suggested Base	Braemar
Accommodation	Hotels at Spittal of Glenshee. Hotels, guest houses and b/b at Braemar, Ballater and Inverey. Youth hostels at Braemar and Muir of Inverey. Caravan site at Ballater.
Public Transport	Rail: London, Glasgow and Edinburgh to Aberdeen for onward bus services to Braemar. Buses: London, Edinburgh, Glasgow and Inverness to Aberdeen for onward bus services to Braemar.

AN SOCACH, 3097FT/944M
CARN BHAC, 3104FT/946M
BEINN IUTHARN MHOR, 3428FT/1045M
CARN AN RIGH, 3376FT/1029M
GLAS TULAICHEAN, 3448FT/1051M

Map: OS Sheet 43: GR 080800, GR 051832,
   GR 045792, GR 028773, GR 051760
Translation: the projecting place; hill of peat hags;
   big hill of the edge; hill of the king; green hills

Pronunciation: *an sochkach; kaarn vachk; byn
yooarn vore; kaarn an ree; glas tooleechan*
Access Point: Inverey, GR 084894
Distance/ascent: 26mls/6000ft; 42km/1829m. This
includes the five mile (8km) walk in each way
from Inverey to Altanour Lodge.
Approx Time: 10-16 hours

⚐ Walk up the length of Glen Ey from Inverey to
Altanour Lodge (ruin). Climb An Socach by
way of its NW ridge, Carn Cruinn, and return
to Altanour. Follow the course of the Allt an
Odhar west and then NW into its shallow
corrie. The summit of the flat-topped Carn
Bhac is only a short distance away to the NW.
From the summit follow the broad ridge SW to
the SW top and follow another broad ridge
south to a broad bealach. From here a steep
climb on heather and scree will take you to the
bald summit ridge of Beinn Iutharn Mhor.
From the cairn continue south and SW,
contouring round the easy slopes of Mam nan
Carn. Reach the low col and climb the steeper
heather slopes to the summit of Carn an Righ.
Retrack to Mam nan Carn and then descend
SSE to the col at the head of Gleann Mor. An
ascent of Glas Tulaichean's north ridge leads to
the summit. Return to Altanour by the north
ridge, Loch nan Eun and descend by the Allt
Beinn Iutharn to the broad valley.

🦌 National Trust for Scotland. No restrictions.

THE CAIRNWELL, 3061ft/933m
CARN A'GHEOIDH, 3199ft/975m
CARN AOSDA, 3008ft/917m

Map: OS Sheet 43: GR 135773, GR 107767,
GR 134792
Translation: From Carn Bhalg, hill of bags; hill of
the goose; hill of age
Pronunciation: cairnwell; kaarn a yowee; kaarn
oesh
Access Point: Devil's Elbow, GR 140780
Distance/ascent: 5mls/1900ft; 8km/579m
Approx Time: 3-5 hours

🐐 Start just south of the ski area and climb heather slopes to the summit. Descend NNW past the top chairlift point and continue on a broad ridge with snow fences. Just before the Cairnwell-Aosda col turn west and drop to another col, the lowest point between The Cairnwell and Carn a'Gheoidh. Continue SW past Carn nan sac and west over a small plateau to Carn a'Gheoidh. Return the way to came to the Cairnwell-Aosda col. From there ascend NE then east along a broad ridge to the flat summit of Carn Aosda. Descend south by bulldozed tracks and roads to the Cairnwell road.

🦌 Invercauld Estate. Tel: 01339-741224.

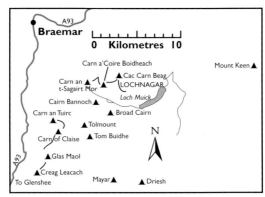

Suggested Base Accommodation	Braemar or Glen Doll Hotels, guest houses and b/b in Braemar, Ballater, Glenshee, Milton of Clova. Youth hostels at Braemar and Glen Doll. Camping/caravan sites at Ballater.
Public Transport	Rail: London, Glasgow and Edinburgh to Dundee and Aberdeen. Buses: Limited transport to southern glens. Aberdeen to Braemar and Ballater. Dundee to Kirriemuir and Blairgowrie for post bus service. Post buses: Kirriemuir to Glen Doll YH, Blairgowrie to Spittal of Glenshee.

GLAS MAOL, 3504FT/1068M
CREAG LEACACH, 3238FT/987M

Map: OS Sheet 43: GR 166765, GR 155746
Translation: green/grey bare hill; slabby rock
Pronunciation: glas moel; krayk lyechach
Access Point: Summit of A93, GR 141799
Distance/ascent: 6mls/1700ft; 10km/518m
Approx Time: 4-6 hours

🐾 Leave the car park at the summit of the
Cairnwell road and climb ski slopes east to the
Meall Odhar ski tows. Keep to the right of the
tow lines, cross Meall Odhar to a flat col.
Continue SW to the great dome of Glas Maol.
Head SW over schistose mossy screes to the
ridge which leads to Creag Leacach. From the
summit continue to the SW top and then turn
NW down a steep slope to the saddle behind
Meall Gorm. From the saddle descend NNE by
a grassy re-entry to the valley below. Head
downstream, cross to the north side of the burn
to a footpath and cross the Allt a'Ghlinne Bhig
by a bridge to reach the A93 a couple of
kilometres south of your starting point.

🦌 Invercauld Estate. Tel: 01339-741224.

CARN AN TUIRC, 3343FT/1019M
CAIRN OF CLAISE, 3491FT/1064M
TOLMOUNT, 3143FT/958M
TOM BUIDHE, 3140FT/957M

Map: OS Sheets 43 and 44: GR 174804,
   GR 185789, GR 210800, GR 214788
Translation: hill of the boar; hill of the follow; hill
   of the valley; yellow hill
Pronunciation: *kaarn an toork; kaarn an claes;*
   tolmount; *tom booee*
Access Point: A93 north of Cairnwell. GR 148800
Distance/ascent: 11mls/2600ft; 18km/792m
Approx Time: 5-8 hours

🐾 Cross the Cairnwell Burn by an ancient bridge
and follow the Allt a'Garbh-coire east on a path
for one kilometre and cross the tributary
coming down from the NE. Climb due east to
the summit of Carn an Tuirc. Continue eas‚t
then as the slope steepens towards Coire
Kander turn SE down a wide and grassy ridge.
Reach a wide saddle below Cairn of Claise and
continue SSE up slopes to the summit. Go ENE
to a peaty col and then up wide slopes to
Tolmount. Descend SW skirting the upper
reaches of a shallow valley and then SE up
grassy slopes to the summit of Tom Buidhe.
From here walk west over Ca Whims, skirt the

slopes of Cairn of Claise on its south side and follow a fence line SW to the route of the Monega Road which follows the spur of Sron na Gaoithe. Leave the ridge on its north side near its termination and follow grass slopes to the Allt a'Garbh-coire and then the bridge at the starting point.

🦌 Invercauld Estate. Tel: 01339-741224 and Balmoral Estate Ranger Tel: 01339-755434.

CARN AN T-SAGAIRT MOR, 3435FT/1047M
CARN A'COIRE BHOIDHEACH, 3668FT/1118M

Map: OS Sheets 43 and 44: GR 208843, GR 226845
Translation: big hill of the priest; hill of the beautiful corrie
Pronunciation: kaarn an takarsht moar; kaarn a corrie vawyach
Access Point: Auchallater on the A93, GR 156882
Distance/ascent: 15mls/2900ft; 24km/884m
Approx Time: 7-10 hours

🐾 Leave Auchallater and follow estate road to Loch Callater Lodge. By the lodge enclosure a path strikes uphill and traverses the hillside above Loch Callater. As it gains height it zig-zags slightly before reaching a bealach below the west slopes of Carn an t-Sagairt Mor. Follow the path up the slopes until it begins to contour to the SE. Leave the path here and climb directly to the summit following a fence line. From the summit continue NE, cross over Carn an t-Sagairt Beag and reach the edge of the plateau. About 500 metres east the Stuic rises and is worth a visit. From there walk another 500 metres over stony tundra to Carn a'Coire Boidheach. Return by the south side of t-Sagairt Mor and Glen Callater.

🦌 Balmoral Estate Ranger. Tel: 01339-755434.

CAIRN BANNOCH, 3320 FT/1012M
BROAD CAIRN, 3274FT/998M

Map: OS Sheet 44: GR 223826, GR 240815
Translation: possibly peaked hill; broad cairn

Pronunciation: kaarn bannoch; broad kaarn
Access Point: Car park in Glen Muick,
  GR 309851
Distance/ascent: 17mls/2400ft; 27km/732m
Approx Time: 8-10 hours

🏃 Leave the car park at the road end in Glen
   Muick and take the bulldozed track on the NE
   shores of Loch Muick. Pass through the Glas-
   allt-Shiel woods and 100 metres after the woods
   take the right fork in the path to follow the Allt
   an Dubh-loch up to its source in the Dubh Loch
   itself. Follow the shore of the loch to its NW
   point and follow the stream which flows down
   from behind creag an Dubh-loch. Continue to
   the summit cone of Cairn Bannoch. Continue
   SE over the undulating plateau to Cairn of
   Gowal and then go east to a broad saddle and
   the gentle climb to Broad Cairn. Continue east
   to reach a rough track which soon becomes a
   bulldozed track. At a wooden shelter continue
   east for 300m then bear left down the path
   which leads to Loch Muick. Follow the path
   along the south shore back to Spittal of
   Glenmuick.
🦌 Balmoral Estate Ranger. Tel: 01339-755434.

LOCHNAGAR, 3789FT/1155M

Map: OS Sheet 44: GR 244862
Translation: named after Lochan na Gaire in NE
  corrie. Little loch of the noisy sound
Pronunciation: loch-na-gar
Access Point: Spittal of Glenmuick car park, GR
  309851
Distance/ascent: 12mls/2700ft; 19km/823m
Approx Time: 5-8 hours

🏃 Take the path which runs along the edge of the
   plantation to cross to the other side of the glen
   at Allt-na-giubhsaich. Take the path which runs
   along the south bank of the burn through the
   pinewoods and reach a track which is followed
   west for about three km to the bealach which
   leads through to Gelder Shiel. At this point take
   an obvious path WSW across a slight hollow

Driesh

and then more steeply to the Foxes' Well on the left of the path. Soon the slope steepens again before 'The Ladder' and the top of the summit ridge. A short descent across a wide col and another climb leads to the flat summit ridge of the mountain. Walk along the rim of the corrie, past Cac Carn Mor and the deep chasm of the Black Spout to the summit cone of Cac Carn Berag where you'll find the trig point. An alternative descent goes via Glas Allt and steep zig-zags to the woods of Glas-allt-Shiel. The track is then followed back to Glen Muick.

🦌 Balmoral Estate Ranger. Tel: 01339-755434.

DRIESH, 3107FT/947M
MAYAR, 3045FT/928M

Map: OS Sheet 44: GR 271736, GR 241738
Translation: from the Gaelic dris, bramble or thorn bush; possibly from m'aighear, my delight, or from magh, a plain
Pronunciation: dreesh; may-yer
Access Point: Braedownie, GR 288757
Distance/ascent: 8mls/2700ft; 13km/823m
Approx Time: 4-6 hours

🏃 Start at the Forestry Commission car park quarter of a mile past Braedownie Farm. A track from Acharn, near the Youth Hostel in Glen Doll, crosses the White Water to a forestry

fence which runs up the hill for just under 1000
feet/305m. Where the fence contours off to the
west continue directly upwards to the top of the
Scorrie where the slopes ease off. Continue to
the summit. From Driesh follow the long and
obvious ridge west for about 3.2km to Mayar.
To descend follow grassy slopes NNE to the
edge of Corrie Fee. Continue on the SE side of
the Fee Burn past small waterfalls to a path at
the foot of one of the steeper sections. Follow
this ENE down the lower corrie, over a stile
and into the forest. The path soon becomes a
forest road which eventually runs past the
Youth Hostel to the FC car park.

🦌 Glenprosen Estate. Tel: 01575-540222.

MOUNT KEEN, 3081FT/939M

Map: OS Sheet 44: GR 409869
Translation: from monadh caoin, smooth or
   pleasant hill
Pronunciation: as spelt
Access Point: Glen Tanar House, GR 473957
Distance/ascent: 15mls/2500ft; 24km/762m
Approx Time: 6-10 hours

🚶 Start at the end of the public road which runs
up Glen Tanar. Walk past a sawmill and
through a gate which leads to an estate road.
Follow this through pinewoods for about 4.8km
and on up the open glen, crossing the river
twice. At the third crossing (GR 407896) ascend
the Mounth Road south by a bulldozed track
through heathery slopes. Diverge SE up the
path to Mount Keen's summit.

🦌 Glen Tanar Estate. Tel: 01339-82451.

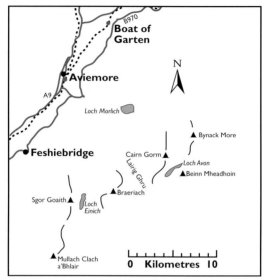

Suggested Base	Kingussie or Aviemore
Accommodation	Hotels, guest houses and b/b in Laggan, Newtonmore, Kingussie, Kincraig, Aviemore, Boat of Garten, Carrbridge and Nethybridge. Youth hostel in Aviemore. Private hostels in Glen Feshie and Newtonmore. Camp sites at Coylumbridge, Loch Morlich, Newtonmore. Caravan sites in Aviemore, Newtonmore, Kingussie and Boat of Garten.
Public Transport	Rail: London, Glasgow and Edinburgh to Inverness. Stations at Kingussie and Aviemore. Buses: London, Glasgow and Edinburgh via Perth to Inverness for Kingussie and Aviemore. Aviemore to

Coire Cas (Cairngorm ski bus
operates all year round).

Mullach Clach a'Bhlair, 3343ft/1019m
Sgor Gaoith, 3668ft/1118m

Map: OS Sheet 43: GR 883927, GR 903989
Translation: summit of the stone of the plain; peak
of the wind
Pronunciation: moolach clach a vaar; skor goo-ee
Access Point: Achlean in Glen Feshie, GR 851972
Distance/ascent: 16mls/2700ft; 26km/823m
Approx Time: 6-8 hours

๛ Leave Achlean in Glen Feshie by the
Foxhunter's Path which climbs Carn Ban Mor
eastwards above the Allt Fhearnagan. Continue
over the shoulder south of Carn Ban Mor until
the footpath joins up with a bulldozed track.
Follow this track SW and south over the Moine
Mhor and past the head of Coire Garbhlach.
Beyond this point another track joins from the
west but continue south and where the track
begins to bend due east leave it and climb the
easy stony slopes of Mullach Clach a'Bhlair.
Return to Carn Ban Mor over the bulldozed
track or wander straight across the Moine Mhor
on bearings. From Carn Ban Mor descend NNE
to the broad bealach above the Fuaran Diotach
then climb the easy slopes of Sgor Gaoith.
Return to Achlean via Carn Ban Mor.

๘ Glen Feshie Estate. Tel: 01479-651324.

Braeriach, 4252ft/1296m

Map: OS Sheets 36 and 43: GR 953999
Translation: brindled upland
Pronunciation: brae-reeach
Access Point: Car park in Coire Cas of
Cairngorm, GR 990061
Distance/ascent: 13mls/2750ft; 21km/838m

๛ Leave the car park by the footpath to Coire an
t-Sneachda. Reach the Sneachda burn and then
head across the heathery moorland west to the
obvious notch of Chalamain Gap. Go through

Cairn Toul and Braeriach

the gap and descend to the Lairig Ghru and the
Sinclair Hut. Climb the hillside behind the hut
by way of the obvious footpath and reach the
broad bealach. Finally climb SW to the edge of
Coire Bhrochain and then follow the corrie lip
to the summit.

🦌 Rothiemurchus Estate. Tel: 01479-810858.

CAIRNGORM, **4085**FT/**1245**M
BEINN MHEADHOIN, **3878**FT/**1182**M

Map: OS Sheet 36: GR 005041, GR 024017
Translation: blue hill; middle hill
Pronunciation: *cairngorom; byn-vee-an*
Access Point: Coire Cas car park, GR 990061
Distance/ascent: 11mls/5500ft; 18km/1676m
Approx Time: 6-10 hours

🐾 Leave the car park and climb Cairngorm by
way of the Sron an Aonaich and the 'Ptarmigan
Bowl'. A dubious alternative is to climb up
through the ski paraphernalia in Coire Cas by
way of bulldozed tracks. From the summit of
Cairngorm descend south into Coire Raibert
and down the steep and loose path beside the
burn to Loch Avon. Follow the path round the
west head of the loch, past the Shelter Stone,
and up into Coire Etchachan. From Loch
Etchachan climb stony slopes NE to the granite
tors of Beinn Mheadhoin. The largest of these is
the summit and can be climbed by an easy

scramble from its north side. Descend steep
slopes, avoiding Creag Dubh, to the foot of
Loch Avon. Cross the steam at its outlet from
the loch and follow the footpath west to the
Saddle at the head of Strath Nethy. Climb the
SE slopes of Cairngorm to Ciste Mhearaid
which is just below the col between Cairngorm
and Cnap Coire na Spreidhe. Return to car
park.

🦌 No restrictions.

Bynack More, 3576ft/1090m

Map: OS Sheet 36: GR 042063
Translation: big cap
Pronunciation: bie-nack moar
Access Point: Glenmore Lodge, GR 992097
Distance/ascent: 12mls/2500ft; 19km/762m
Approx Time: 5-8 hours

🦌 Leave parking area just beyond Glenmore
Lodge and follow the forestry track into the
Pass of Ryvoan. Continue through the Pass,
past Lochan Uaine. Quarter of a mile beyond
the lochan take another path east to Bynack
Stable and the River Nethy. Cross the river and
follow the footpath SE over the lower shoulder
of Bynack More. Follow this path to its highest
point then leave it to bear south up the north
ridge to the summit. Return the same way or by
Strath Nethy.

🦌 Scottish Natural Heritage. Tel: 01479-810287.

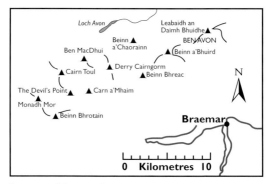

Suggested Base	Braemar
Accommodation	Hotels at Spittal of Glenshee, hotels, guest houses and b/b at Braemar, Ballater and Inverey. Youth Hostels at Braemar and Inverey. Private Hostel at Braemar. Caravan/camping site at Braemar.
Public Transport	Rail: London, Glasgow and Edinburgh to Aberdeen for onward bus service to Braemar. Buses: London, Edinburgh, Glasgow and Inverness to Aberdeen for onward bus service to Braemar.

THE DEVIL'S POINT, 3294FT/1004M
CAIRN TOUL, 4242FT/1293M

Map: OS Sheets 36 and 43: GR 976951, GR 964972

Translation: from original name of hill Bod an Deamhain, penis of the devil; from carn an t-sabhail, hill of the barn

Pronunciation: as spelt; *kaarn towal*

Access Point: Linn of Dee, GR 061897

Distance/ascent: 23mls/3700ft; 37km/1128m

Approx Time: 8-12 hours

Looking across the An Garbh Coire to Cairn Toul from Braeriach

🐾 Take the private road from Linn of Dee to Derry Lodge. Follow the track up Glen Luibeg to the Lairig Ghru. Follow the path which skirts the southern slops of Carn a'Mhaim and drops to Glen Dee. Cross the river to Corrour Bothy. A worn path leads west behind the bothy up steep zig-zags above the Allt a'Choire Odhair. From the col at the head of the corrie head south then bear east to the summit The Devil's Point. Return to the col. Follow the broad grassy ridge which rises north. Follow the ridge to Stob Coire an t-Saighdeir and then to Cairn Toul.

🦌 National Trust for Scotland. No restrictions.

MONADH MOR, 3651FT/1113M
BEINN BHROTAIN, 3816FT/1163M

Map: OS Sheet 43: GR 938942, GR 954923
Translation: big hill; hill of the mastiff
Pronunciation: monagh moar; byn vrotan
Access Point: Linn of Dee, GR 061897
Distance/ascent: 23mls/3000ft; 37km/914m
Approx Time: 8-12 hours

  ᴁ Take the private road west from Linn of Dee to
White Bridge. Continue past the Chest of Dee
and along the path to its end. Take to the rough
moor and enter Glen Geusachan. Follow the
stream up the glen and climb to the outflow
from Loch nan Stuirteag. Turn south and climb
the obvious ridge of Monadh Mor to the
summit, Head south to another top at
3642ft/1110m and then descend SE above the
head of Coire Cath nam Fionn. From the col
continue SE to the summit of Beinn Bhrotain.
Continue SE over Carn Cloich-mhuilinn and
down its east ridge to Glen Dee.

  ❦ National Trust for Scotland. No restrictions.

BEN MACDUI, 4295FT/1309M
CARN A'MHAIM, 3402FT/1037M
DERRY CAIRNGORM, 3789FT/1155M

Map: OS Sheets 36 and 43: GR 988989,
    GR 994952, GR 017980
Translation: hill of the black pig; cairn of the
    large round hill; blue hill of Derry (from doire;
    a thicket)
*Pronunciation: byn macdooee; kaarn a vame;
    derry cairngorom*
Access Point: Linn of Dee, GR 061897
Distance/ascent: 19mls/4500ft; 30km/1372m
Approx Time: 8-12 hours

  ᴁ Take the private road from Linn of Dee to
Derry Lodge. Cross the Derry Burn by the
bridge west of Derry Lodge. Follow the track to
the Luibeg Bridge and then leave the track to
climb the SE ridge of Carn a'Mhaim. The NW
top is the summit. From here follow the

narrowing ridge in a NNW direction to a wide
col at 2625 ft/800m. Climb the steep and stony
slopes due north to the summit of Beinn
Macdui. Descend east over wide bouldery and
featureless slopes to the edge of Coire Sputan
Dearg and follow the ridge NE to a col just west
of Creagan a Choire Etchachan. Skirting the
SW slopes of Creagan a Choire Etchachan
descend south to the bealach north of Derry
Cairngorm. Climb bouldery slopes south to the
summit. Return to Derry Lodge by Carn Crom.
🦌 National Trust for Scotland. No restrictions.

BEINN BHREAC, 3054FT/931M
BEINN A'CHAORAINN, 3550FT/1082M

Map: OS Sheets 36 and 43: GR 058971,
   GR 045013
Translation: speckled hill; hill of the rowan
Pronunciation: *byn vrechk; byn a choeran*
Access Point: Linn of Dee, GR 061897
Distance/ascent: 18mls/2700ft; 29km/823m
Approx Time: 7-10 hours

🥾 Take the private road to Derry Lodge.
Continue on the bulldozed track on the east
side of Glen Derry for just over a mile then
strike uphill over heathery slopes and through
trees to the col between Meall an Lundain and
Beinn Bhreac. From here climb NNE to the
summit. Continue NW then north across the
Moine Bhealaidh to Beinn a'Chaorainn. Return
to Derry Lodge by the Lairig an Laoigh track.
🦌 National Trust for Scotland. No restrictions.

BEN AVON, LEABAIDH AN DAIMH BHUIDHE, 3842FT/1171M
BEINN A'BHUIRD, 3924FT/1196M

Map: OS Sheets 36 and 43: GR 132019,
   GR 093006
Translation: bed of the yellow stag; hill of the
   table
Pronunciation: *lyepay an dyv vooee; byn a voord*
Access Point: Invercauld Bridge, GR 186909
Distance/ascent: 25mls/4500ft; 40km/1372m
Approx Time: 11-15 hours

   ** Leave your car at Keiloch and continue on the private road to Glen Quoich. Continue past the ruins of Slugain Lodge to the end of the path beyond the boulder of Clach a'Chleirich. From there climb NNE to the obvious saddle at 3182ft/970m called The Sneck. From here climb east up gravelly slopes to the summit of Beinn Avon, Leabaidh an Daimh Bhuidhe. Return to the Sneck, cross it and continue ESE over featureless plateau to the North Top of Beinn a'Bhuird. Return to Glen Quoich by the south top and carn Fiaclach where a stalkers' path takes you back to just north of Slugain Lodge.

   ૎ Invercauld Estate. Tel: 01339-741224.

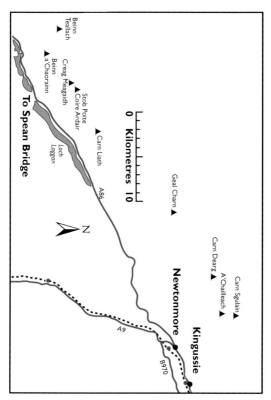

Suggested Base	Newtonmore
Accommodation	Hotels, guest houses and b/b at Newtonmore and Laggan. Private Bunkhouse in Newtonmore. Caravan site at Glen Truim and caravan/camping site at Newtonmore.
Public Transport	Rail: London, Glasgow and Edinburgh to Inverness. Station at Newtonmore. Bus to Laggan,

Roybridge and Fort William.
Buses: London, Glasgow and
Edinburgh to Inverness,
stopping at Newtonmore.

CARN DEARG, 3100FT/945M
A'CHAILLEACH, 3051FT/930M
CARN SGULAIN, 3018FT/920M

Map: OS Sheet 35: GR 635024, GR 681042,
GR 684059
Translation: red hill; the old woman; hill of the
basket or of the old man
*Pronunciation: kaarn jerrag; a kaalyach; kaarn
skoolin*
Access Point: Glen Banchor, GR 693998
Distance/ascent: 15mls/2750ft; 24km/838m
Approx Time: 6-8 hours

Drive up Glen Banchor to the parking area
above Shepherd's Bridge. Follow the footpath
north beside the Allt a'Chaorainn till it ends in
a turning point. Drop down to the stream and
cross by a footbridge which is hidden from the
path. Climb heathery slopes NNE to the
rounded summit of A'Chailleach. Descend
north into a deep glen and then continue north
on steep and tussocky grass to the summit of
Carn Sgulain. From the summit follow a line of
fence posts west then SW over undulating
plateau crossing several minor tops. At Carn
Ban leave the fence posts and go south to a
short and steep climb to the summit of Carn
Dearg. From here continue on the narrow ridge
south to a bealach and drop east into Gleann
Balloch down broad heathery slopes. A narrow
footpath follows the stream back into Glen
Banchor from where another track beside the
River Calder takes you back to Shepherd's
Bridge.

Banchor Mains Farm. Tel: 01479-673215.

GEAL CHARN, 3038FT/926M

Map: OS Sheet 35: GR 561988
Translation: white hill

Pronunciation: gyal chaarn
Access Point: Garva Bridge, GR 521948
Distance/ascent: 9mls/2000ft; 14km/610m
Approx Time: 4-6 hours

ᚥ From the bridge follow the path which runs up
the SE side of the Feith Talagain. At the end of
the path cross the Allt Coire nan Dearcag and
climb the heather covered SW ridge of Geal
Charn direct to the summit. Return by Beinn
Sgiath and the SW ridge.

ᛏ West Highland Estates Office, Fort William.
Tel: 01397-702433.

CREAG MEAGAIDH, 3707FT/1130M
CARN LIATH, 3300FT/1006M
STOB POITE COIRE ARDAIR, 3455FT/1053M

Map: OS Sheets 34 and 42: GR 418875,
GR 472904, GR 429889
Translation: bogland rock; grey hill; peak of the
pot of the high corrie
*Pronunciation: krayk meggie; kaarn leea; stop
potya kor aardar*
Access Point: Aberarder Farm, GR 482872
Distance/ascent: 16mls/4500ft; 26km/1372m
Approx Time: 8-12 hours

ᚥ Behind the Scottish Natural Heritage buildings
at Aberarder Farm a good path crosses the
lower moorland. After a mile or so, as the track
climbs through birch trees strike uphill NNE on
the heather clad slopes of Carn Liath. From the
summit head NW to follow the edge of Coire
Ardair over Meall an t-Snaim, Sron Garbh
Choire and the east top of Stob Poite Coire
Ardair. Continue west to the summit. From the
cairn continue west then south as the slopes fall
way to 'The Window', a deep col. Climb the
steep slopes on to the plateau, past Mad Meg's
Cairn to the true summit. Leave the cairn
behind and walk east to the edge of the corrie
and follow the ridge SE and east over Puist
Coire Ardair and Creag Mhor. Drop down open
slopes to Aberarder.

ᛏ Scottish Natural Heritage. Tel: 01479-810287.

BEINN TEALLACH, 3002FT/915M
BEINN A'CHAORUINN, 3451FT/1052M

Map: OS Sheets 34 and 41: GR 361860,
   GR 386851
Translation: forge hill; hill of the rowan
Pronunciation: byn tyellach; byn a choerin
Access Point: Roughburn, GR 377813
Distance/ascent: 11mls/3750ft; 18km/1143m
Approx Time: 4-7 hours

🐾 Follow the forestry road NW for 800 metres to
   the slopes below Meall Clachaig. Follow a
   firebreak north to reach a deer fence and a gate
   near the road junction. Climb north and then
   bear NE up easy slopes to the south top and
   then along the broad ridge to the summit of
   Beinn a'Chaoruinn. Continue on the ridge to
   the north top and then drop NNW, then west to
   the col at the head of the Allt a'Chaoruinn.
   Climb the slopes west to reach the NE ridge of
   beinn Teallach. Follow the ridge to the summit.
🦌 Fountain Forestry. Tel: 01463-224948.

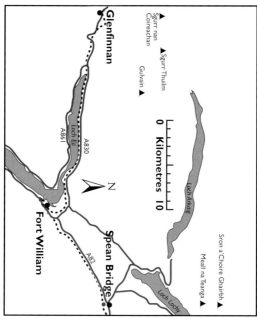

Suggested Base Accommodation	Spean Bridge Hotels, guest houses and b/b at Spean Bridge, Roybridge, Fort William, Invergarry. Youth Hostel at Fort William (Glen Nevis) and Loch Lochy. Camping/caravan sites at Spean Bridge, Roybridge and Invergarry.
Public Transport	Rail: Glasgow to Mallaig. Station at Spean Bridge. Buses: Oban and Fort William to Inverness for Laggan Locks and Loch Lochy.

Sron a'Choire Ghairbh, 3067ft/935m
Meall na Teanga, 3008ft/917m

Map: OS Sheet 34: GR 223945, GR 220924
Translation: nose of the rough corrie; hill of the
    tongue
Pronunciation: *srawn a corrie ghirav; myowl na
    tyenga*
Access Point: North end of Loch Lochy, GR
    287963
Distance/ascent: 13mls/4250ft; 21km/1295m
Approx Time: 6-9 hours

* At the north end of Loch Lochy cross by the
    Laggan Locks to Kilfillan. Follow the Forestry
    Commission track SW above the loch. After
    about 3km follow a track which climbs from the
    forest track uphill NW then west to the obvious
    pass between the two hills. From the top of the
    pass, climb Meall na Teanga first, return to the
    head of the pass then climb Sron a'Choire
    Ghairbh. Descend by the latter's long eastern
    spur directly to Kilfillan.
* Forestry Commission. Tel: 01320-366322.

Gulvain, 3238ft/987m

Map: OS Sheets 40 and 41: GR 003876
Translation: from Gaor Bheinn, possibly filthy hill
Pronunciation: *goolvan*
Access Point: Drumsallie, GR 960794
Distance/ascent: 12mls/3700ft; 19km/1128m
Approx Time: 6-8 hours

* Start from Drumsallie on the A830 Fort William
    to Mallaig road and follow the track up the east
    side of the Fionn Lighe river. Continue up the
    glen for about 5.6km till you reach the foot of
    the SSE ridge of Gulvain. Climb the ridge, past
    a craggy knoll and the south top and climb the
    narrowing ridge to the summit.
* Locheil Estates. Tel: 01397-702433.

SGURR THUILM, 3159FT/963M
SGURR NAN COIREACHAN, 3136FT/956M

Map: OS Sheet 40: GR 939879, GR 903880
Translation: peak of the round hillock; peak of
the corries
Pronunciation: skoor hoolim; skoor nam
korachan
Access Point: Glenfinnan, GR 905809
Distance/ascent: 12mls/4000ft; 19km/1219m
Approx Time: 6-9 hours

⚥ Follow the private road up the right side of the
River Finnan below the railway viaduct. Just
over three km up the glen pass the Corryhully
bothy and continue on the track until it crosses
the stream that drains Coire Thollaidh and
Coire a'Bheithe. Cross the stream and head for
the obvious spur that leads to Druim Coire
a'Bheithe and the summit of Sgurr Thuilm.
From the cairn return south for a short
distance to join the main ridge which runs west
over the ups and downs of Beinn Gharbh and
Meall an Tarmachain to the final climb to Sgurr
nan Coireachan. From the summit descend SE
and then climb to Sgurr a'Choire Riabhaich
where the ridge becomes very steep-sided and
care should be taken. Follow the ridge to the
track NE of the Corryhully Bothy.
🏶 Glenfinnan Estate. Tel: 01397-722270.

Gulvain

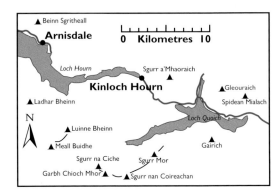

Suggested Base	Invergarry
Accommodation	Hotels, guest houses and b/b at Invergarry, Spean Bridge, Sheil Bridge and Tomdoun. Private hostel at Inverie. Private bothy at Barrisdale.
Public Transport	Rail: Glasgow to Mallaig. Stations at Spean Bridge and Fort William for onward bus services. Mallaig for ferry to Inverie. Buses: Glasgow to Skye. Edinburgh and Perth to Skye for Invergarry. Fort William to Inverness for Invergarry. Post buses: Invergarry to Kinloch Hourn for Loch Quoich-side. Kyle of Lochalsh to Arnisdale for ferry to Barrisdale on Knoydart. Ferries: Arnisdale to Kinloch Hourn for Barrisdale, Mallaig to Inverie on Loch Nevis.

SGURR NA CICHE, 3415FT/1041M
GARBH CHIOCH MHOR, 3323FT/1013M

Map: OS Sheets 33 and 40: GR 902966,
  GR 909961

Translation: peak of the breast; big rough place of
  the breast

Pronunciation: skoor na keesh; garav kee-ach
  voar

Access Point: Strathan, GR 979915

Distance/ascent: 13mls/3000ft; 21km/914m

Approx Time: 6-8 hours

Follow the track from Strathan to Glen
Dessarry. Take the uphill path behind the
house of Upper Glendessarry to reach the Allt
Coire nan Uth and climb diagonally uphill to
reach the saddle of Bealach nan Gall. Climb
west up increasingly rocky slopes to the ridge
which leads to Garbh Chioch Bheag and then
Garbh Choich Mhor. Beyond the summit the
ridge narrows considerably on the descent to
Feadan na Ciche. From the pass take the
obvious grassy ramp which leads to a succession
of grassy ledges which lead through the rocky
screes and blocks to the summit rib. From the
summit return to the Feadan Gap. From here
descend SW down the course of the Allt Coire
Ciche, steep in places to a grassy terrace from
which easy slopes drop down to the Mam na
Cloich' Airde pass. Follow the path back to

Gharbh Chioch Mhor and Sgurr na Ciche

Glen Dessarry and Strathan.
🦌 Tel: 01738-628151.

SGURR NAN COIREACHAN, 3127FT/953M
SGURR MOR, 3290FT/1003M

Map: OS Sheets 33 and 40: GR 933958,
   GR 965980
Translation: peak of the corries; big peak
Pronunciation: skoor nan korachan; skoor mor
Access Point: Strathan, GR 979915
Distance/ascent: 14mls/5000ft; 22km/1524m
Approx Time: 9-10 hours

🚶 Take the Glen Dessarry track to where it
   crosses the Allt Coire nan Uth. Climb the
   mountain's southern slopes directly to a cairned
   top. The main summit is a little to the north.
   An ancient fence bounds the head of Coire nan
   Uth and this should be followed. The ridge
   continues to An Eag and then NE along another
   ridge which drops to a bealach and then climbs
   Sgurr Beag. Beyond another small dip in the
   ridge a 600ft/183m climb takes you to the
   summit of Sgurr Mor.
🦌 Tel: 01738-628151.

GAIRICH, 3015FT/919M

Map: OS Sheet 33: GR 025995
Translation: roaring
Pronunciation: gaareech
Access Point: Loch Quoich dam, GR 069024
Distance/ascent: 9mls/2500ft; 14km/762m
Approx Time: 4-6 hours

🚶 From the south end of the dam a path leads to
   an old stalkers' path which runs south over
   boggy moorland to the edge of a forestry
   plantation. Here another path runs due west,
   up the Druim na Geld Salaich. Once the broad
   ridge crest is reached the path peters out. The
   going is easy however, and the broad ridge
   should be followed west to the final steep pull to
   Gairich. At the foot of this final rise a path
   reappears, but after a while it runs out on to

Sgurr nan Coireachan from Sgurr Thuilm

the south face. Don't be tempted by it but continue climbing on the crest of the ridge to the spacious summit and large cairn.

🦌 Forestry Commission. Tel: 01397-702184.

LUINNE BHEINN, **3080**FT**/939**M
MEALL BUIDHE, **3104**FT**/946**M

Map: OS Sheets 33 and 40: GR 868008, GR 849990
Translation: hill of anger or hill of melody; yellow hill
Pronunciation: loonya vyn; myowl booee
Access Point: Barrisdale, GR 872043
Distance/ascent: 12mls/4500ft; 19km/1372m
Approx Time: 6-9 hours

🦌 Take the Inverie path to the head of Mam Barrisdale. Above the pass, the NW ridge of Luinne Bheinn drops down in a sharp even line. Follow this ridge to the summit. At the east end of Luinne Bheinn a steep southern flank drops to a broad knolly ridge which eventually forms Druim Leac a'Shith. This ridge borders a remote and desolate north corrie of Meall Buidhe. Follow this ridge, over its complex bumps and knolls, and climb gradually to the more obvious defined NE ridge of Meall Buidhe which takes you to the east summit. The true summit is a few hundred yards to the west.

🦌 Tel: 01796-481355.

LADHAR BHEINN, 3346FT/1020M

Map: OS Sheet 33: GR 824040
Translation: hoof or claw hill
Pronunciation: laarven
Access Point: Barrisdale, GR 872043
Distance/ascent: 9mls/3500ft; 14km/1067m
Approx Time: 4-6 hours

🚶 A bridge crosses the river above Barrisdale to a
path which in turn crosses the saltings to meet a
stalkers' path below Creag Bheithe. Follow this
path up zig-zags, round the nose of Creag
Bheithe and through some woodland into Coire
Dhorrcail. Cross the Allt Coire Dhorrcail and
climb grassy slopes west to the ridge of Druim
a'Choire Odhair. Follow this narrowing ridge to
the crest of Stob a'Choire Odhair, then on to
the summit ridge of Ladhar Bheinn. A cairn at
this point is often mistaken for the summit, but
the true summit lies a few hundred yards to the
west. To complicate matters further an OS trig
point lies at the western end of the ridge at a
height of 3313 feet. The best descent lies SE,
over the ridges above Coire Dhorrcail and
Coire na Cabaig, over Aonach Sgoilte and down
the east ridge to Mam Barrisdale.
🦌 Tel: 01796-481355.

BEINN SGRITHEALL, 3195FT/974M

Map: OS Sheet 33: GR 836126
Translation: hill of screes
Pronunciation: byn skreehal
Access Point: Opposite Eilean Rarsaidh on the
    Arnisdale road, GR 815120
Distance/ascent: 6mls/3200ft; 10km/975m
Approx Time: 4-6 hours

🚶 Follow the old hill track to Glenelg up through
some scattered woods and make for an obvious
break in the rocky escarpment above you.
Above the crags turn right and cross some
moorland with scattered lochans. The west

Coire Dhorrcail of Ladhar Bheinn

ridge of Sgritheall is now quite obvious and leads to the summit. Continue east on the ridge which soon narrows again. Follow it to the Bealach Arnisdale; a stream offers the best guide back to Arnisdale itself and the Loch Hourn road.

🦌 Tel: 01599-522244.

SGURR A'MHAORAICH, 3369FT/1027M

Map: OS Sheet 33: GR 984065
Translation: peak of the shellfish
Pronunciation: skoor a vooreach
Access Point: Quoich Bridge, GR 014040
Distance/ascent: 7mls/3200ft; 11km/975m
Approx Time: 4-6 hours

🐾 Follow a stalkers' path which starts just SW of the bridge. Follow the path north up the ridge of Bac nan Canaichean to Sgur Coire nan Eireallach and then across a slight dip to its NW top. From here another ridge leads west to the summit of Sgurr a'Mhaoraich.

🦌 Tel: 01796-481355.

GLEOURAICH, 3396FT/1035M
SPIDEAN MIALACH, 3268FT/996M

Map: OS Sheet 33: GR 039054, GR 066043
Translation: uproar or noise; peak of wild animals
Pronunciation: glyawreech; speetyan meealach

Access Point: Loch Quoich, GR 029030
Distance/ascent: 7mls/3600ft; 11km/1097m
Approx Time: 4-6 hours

🐾 A cairn on the west side of the Allt Coire
Peitireach indicates the beginning of what
becomes a very good stalkers' path. Above the
300-metres contour the path moves on to a
grassy spur and then zig-zags uphill and
continues all the way to the rocky crest of the
hill. A wide stony ridge continues east, drops
and then rises to Craig Coire Fiar Bhealaich.
Beyond another stalkers' path zig-zags down to
the Fiar Bhealaich and then another climb
brings you to the summit of Spidean Mialach.
Descend easy slopes to the SW, passing Loch
Fearna and down the slopes of Coire Mheil to
the roadside.

🦌 Tel: 01796-481355.

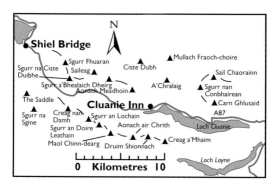

Suggested Base	Shiel Bridge
Accommodation	Hotels, guest houses and b/b at Shiel Bridge, Dornie, Cluanie and Glenelg. Youth Hostel at Ratagan.
Public Transport	Rail: Inverness to Kyle of Lochalsh. Onward bus services. Buses: Kyle of Lochalsh and Plockton to Shiel Bridge and Letterfearn. Glasgow and Fort William to Skye. Edinburgh and Perth to Skye. Inverness to Skye; all stopping at Shiel Bridge. Post buses: Kyle of Lochalsh to Arnisdale for Shiel Bridge.

THE SADDLE, 3314FT/1010M
SGURR NA SGINE, 3100FT/945M

Map: OS Sheet 33: GR 936131, GR 946113
Translation: peak of the knife
Pronunciation: as spelt; *skoor na skeenya*
Access Point: Achnagart, GR 968142
Distance/ascent: 10mls/4700ft; 16km/1433m
Approx Time: 5-7 hours

The Forcan Ridge of The Saddle

🏃 Start SE of the quarry at Achnagart. A stalkers' path leads west to a bealach between Biod an Fhithich and Meallan Odhar. From here go south then SW to the bottom of the Saddle's east ridge, known as the Forcan Ridge. Follow this ridge, knife edged and exposed in places to Sgurr na Forcan. Continue west down a steep rock pitch with good holds and traverse a narrow ridge to the east top of the Saddle and then the summit. The OS trig point is further on and lower than the cairn which marks the summit. Descend to the Bealach Coire Mhalagain down rough bouldery slopes and climb to the NW top o Sgurr na Sgine. Follow a rocky ridge SE to the summit cairn. Descend by way of Faochag and its fine NE ridge.

🦌 No number given.

THE SOUTH GLEN SHEIL RIDGE:
CREAG A'MHAIM, 3107FT/947M
DRUIM SHIONNACH, 3238FT/987M
AONACH AIR CHRITH, 3350FT/1021M
MAOL CHINN-DEARG, 3218FT/981M
SGURR AN DOIRE LEATHAIN, 3314FT/1010M
SGURR AN LOCHAIN, 3294FT/1004M
CREAG NAN DAMH, 3012FT/918M

Map: OS Sheet 33: GR 088078, GR 074085, GR 051083, GR 032088 GR 015099, GR 005104, GR 983112

Translation: rock of the large round hill; ridge of
the fox; trembling hill; bald red hill; peak of
the broad thicket; peak of the little loch; rock
of the stags

Pronunciation: *crayk a vaim; drim heeanach;
oenach ayr chree; moel chan dyerack; skoor an
dira lethan; skoor an lochan; krayk nam dav*

Access Point: Cluanie Inn, GR 075118

Distance/ascent: 15mls/6000ft; 24km/1829m

Approx Time: 7-11 hours

⚲ Take the old road from Cluanie Inn to Glen
Loyne and climb Creag a'Mhaim by the streams
which flow down Coirean an Eich Bhric. Follow
the broad ridge NW to Druim Shionnach,
descend a short dip then a gradual rise brings
you to Aonach air Chrith. This is the high point
of the ridge. Continue now on the narrowest
section of the ridge towards Maol Chinn-dearg.
On the north spur of this hill a stalkers' path
runs into Coire Chuil Droma Bhig, offering a
convenient exit for those who would rather split
the ridge into two days walking. Continue NW
to the minor top of Sgurr Coire na Feinne, then
west to the flat topped Sgurr an Doire Leathain.
From here the ridge dips again, before rising to
Sgurr an Lochain. Another minor top follows,
Sgurr Beag, although this top can be contoured
on its south side to reach the col before the last
Munro of the ridge, Creag nan Damh. From
here a fence leads west to the Bealach Duibh
Leac and a stalkers' path to Glen Shiel.

✓ No contact available.

FIVE SISTERS OF KINTAIL:
SGURR NA CISTE DUIBHE, 3369FT/1027M
SGURR FHUARAN, 3504FT/1068M

Map: OS Sheet 33: GR 984149, GR 978167

Translation: peak of the black chest; meaning
obscure

Pronunciation: *skoor na keesta ghoo; skoor
ooaran*

Access Point: Glensheil Bridge, GR 990132

Distance/ascent: 10mls/5000ft; 16km/1524m

Approx Time: 6-8 hours

🦌 From Glenshiel Bridge climb the steep and
unrelenting slopes of Sgurr na Ciste Duibhe.
Make for the ridge west of Sgurr nan
Spainteach. From here follow the narrow ridge
west to Sgurr na Ciste Duibhe's summit.
Avoiding a false ridge which runs north of the
peak continue NW and descend to the Bealach
na Craoibhe. Turn north and climb over Sgurr
na Carnach to a V-shaped gap of the Bealach
na Carnach. From here a short and steep
ascent leads to the summit of Sgurr Fhuaran. A
descent can be made from here by the east
ridge to Glenlicht House but most walkers
continue north for the full traverse, over Sgurr
nan Saighead and down the NW spur to Sgurr
an t-Searrach from where steep rough slopes
lead to the cottages at Shiel Bridge.

🦌 National Trust for Scotland. No restrictions.

SAILEAG, 3146FT/959M
SGURR A'BHEALAICH DHEIRG, 3405FT/1038M
AONACH MEADHOIN, 3291FT/1003M
CISTE DHUBH, 3222FT/982M

Map: OS Sheet 33: GR 017148, GR 035143,
  GR 049137, GR 062166
Translation: little heel; peak of the red pass;
  middle hill; black chest
Pronunciation: saalak; skoor a vyaleech yerak;
  oenach vain; keesta doo
Access Point: Glenlicht House, GR 005173
Distance/asent: 11mls/5500ft; 18km/1676m
Approx Time: 6-8 hours. The walk-in to Glenlicht
  House from Croe Bridge is four miles (6.5km)

🦌 From Glenlicht House climb SE up the grassy
wall of Meall a'Charra, then up the long grassy
spur which leads to Saileag. Follow the ridge
east above the Fraoch-choire where a sweeping
rise takes you to sgurr a'Bhealaich Dheirg. The
summit cairn likes about 50 metres north of the
main ridge. Return to the ridge and continue
ESE to Aonach Meadhoin and a short narrow
section of ridge to another top on Sgurr an
Fhuarail. A wide ridge now runs north and dips
to a green bealach. Above this pass a steep and

narrow ridge runs north to Ciste Dhubh from where the NW ridge can be desceded to the Allt Cam-ban. This can be difficult to cross in times of spate.

🦌 National Trust for Scotland. No restrictions.

A'CHRALAIG, 3674FT/1120M
MULLACH FRAOCH-CHOIRE, 3615FT/1102M

Map: OS Sheets 33 and 34: GR 094148,
  GR 095171
Translation: basket or creel; heather-corrie peak
Pronunciation: a chraalik; moolach froech-chora
Access Point: West end of Loch Cluanie,
  GR 089121
Distance/ascent: 8mls/3500ft; 13km/1067m
Approx Time: 5-8 hours

🚶 Leave the A87 near the west end of Loch Cluanie where a stalkers' track leaves the road to run through the An Caorrann Mor to Glen Affric. Don't follow the track but climb steeply NE up grassy slopes on A'Chralaig. Continue until the angle eases on the south ridge, and follow this ridge to the large summit cairn. Continue north along a grassy ridge and cross the top of Stob Coire na Cralaig. After this the ridge narrows considerably and several pinnacles have to be crossed before reaching the summit of Mullach. Either return to the start the way you came, or alternatively drop down into Coire Odhar (steep at first) and return by the track in An Caorrann Mor.
🦌 Ceannacroc Estate. Tel: 01320-340243.

CARN GHLUASAID, 3140FT/957M
SGURR NAN CONBHAIREAN, 3642FT/1110M
SAIL CHAORAINN, 3287FT/1002M

Map: OS Sheet 34: GR 146125, GR 130139,
  GR 134155
Translation: hill of movement; peak of the keeper
  of the hounds; hill (heel) of the rowan
*Pronunciation: kaarn ghlooasat; skoor nan
  konavaran; sale choeran*
Access Point: Lundie, Loch Cluanie, GR 145105

Distance/ascent: 10mls/3500ft; 16km/1067m
Approx Time: 6-8 hours

🐾 Leave the A87 at Lundie, about 2.5 miles (4km)
west of Cluanie dam. Follow the old military
road west for a few hundred metres then follow
the obvious and well-constructed stalkers' path
which climbs the south slopes of Carn
Ghluasaid all the way on to its extensive
plateau. Cross the plateau to the summit which
sits fairly close to the edge of the north face.
continue west then NW along the broad ridge,
crossing Creag a'Chaorainn then west to cross a
col and the final climb to Sgurr nan
Conbhairean. From here descend north down
an easy ridge to a col and climb Sail Chaorainn
by its easy angled SSW ridge. To return follow
the ridge back towards Conbhairean but bypass
the summit on its west side. Continue SW to a
col above Gorm Lochan and continue a short
distance to Drochaid an Tuill Easaich. (A 'Top'
unnamed on the 1:50,000 map). Descend the
south ridge back to the old military road which
will take you back to Lundie.

🦌 Ceannacroc Estate. Tel: 01320-340243.

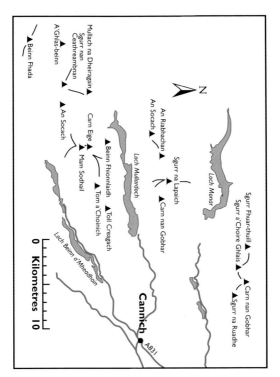

Suggested Base Accommodation	Shiel Bridge or Cannich Hotels, guest houses and b/b in Shiel Bridge, Dornie, Kyle of Lochalsh, Cannich, Tomich. Youth Hostels at Ratagan, Cannich and Alltbeigh. Camping/caravan sites at Beauly, Muir of Ord and Drumnadrochit.
Public Transport	Rail: Inverness to Wick and Thurso, and Inverness to Kyle of Lochalsh. Station at Muir of Ord for onward post bus

service. Buses: Inverness to
Dingwall, Tain and Dornoch.
Inverness to Garve and Ullapool
for Beauly and Muir of Ord for
onward post bus service. Post
buses: Beauly to Tomich for
Struy and Cannich. Muir of Ord
to Sthrathconon for
Inverchoran.

A'GHLAS-BHEINN, 3012FT/918M

Map: OS Sheet 33: GR 008231
Translation: greenish-grey hill
Pronunciation: a'glasvin
Access Point: Strath Croe, GR 977222
Distance/ascent: 8mls/3000ft; 13km/914m
Approx Time: 4-6 hours

🐾 Leave the car park near Dorusduain and take
the path which climbs to the Bealach na Sroine.
Just beyond the top of the bealach climb south
on the slopes of Meall Dubh, steeply at first and
then easing off considerably. Continue SSW
over a knobbly ridge to the summit. to descend
continue south down easy, then steeper slopes
to the Bealach an Sgairne and a delightful
stalkers' path which carries you all the way
back to the start.

🦌 Inverinate Estate. Tel: 01599-588262.

BEINN FHADA (BEN ATTOW), 3386FT/1032M

Map: OS Sheet 33: GR 018192
Translation: long hill
Pronunciation: byn ata
Access Point: Strath Croe, GR 977222
Distance/ascent: 11mls/3750ft; 18km/1143m
Approx Time: 6-8 hours

🐾 From the car park near Dorusduain take the
stalker's path which runs up to the Bealach an
Sgairne. After crossing the stream which flows
down from Coire an Sgairne take another path
which runs up into the corrie and climb the
slopes of Meall a'Bhealaich. Follow this ridge

Looking towards Mam Sodhail and Carn Eige

south to where it abuts on to the great summit
plateau of Beinn Fhada known as the Plaide
Mor. Continue SE along the edge of the plateau
to the summit cairn.

🦌 National Trust for Scotland. No restrictions.

AN SOCACH, 3018FT/920M
SGURR NAN CEATHREAMHNAN, 3776FT/1151M
MULLACH NA DHEIRAGAIN, 3222FT/982M

Map: OS Sheets 25 and 33: GR 088230,
  GR 057228, GR 081259
Translation: the snout; peak of the quarters;
  possibly summit of the hawk
Pronunciation: *an sochkach; skoor nan
  keroanan; moollach na yerakan*
Access Point: Alltbeithe, GR 080202
Distance/ascent: 16mls/5500ft; 26km/1676m
Approx Time: 7-12 hours

🐾 Reach the Alltbeithe Youth Hostel from either
Loch Beinn a'Mheadhoin in Glen Affric
(10mls/16km) or a shorter route through the An
Caorrann Mor from Cluanie. From Alltbeithe a
footpath beside the Allt na Faing leads directly
to the ridge just west of An Socach. Go east to
the summit. Return to the ridge and follow it
west again. Climb grassy terraces to the top of
Stob Coire nan Dearcag. Continue on the gently
rising ridge to the east top of Ceathreamhnan.
Continue over rocky ground to the summit.

Rough ground to the NE of the summit leads to
a descent to a sharp rib above An Gorm-
lochan. The ridge now broadens and offers an
easy walk along the length of Creag
a'Choir'Aird to Mullach na Dheiragain. Return
to Ceathreamhnan and descend to Alltbeithe by
the south ridge of the west top.

🦌 National Trust for Scotland. No restrictions.

TOLL CREAGACH, 3458FT/1054M
TOM A'CHOINICH, 3645FT/1111M
CARN EIGE (EIGHE), 3881FT/1183M
BEINN FHIONNLAIDH, 3297FT/1005M
MAM SODHAIL (MAM SOUL), 3871FT/1180M

Map: OS Sheet: 25: GR 194283, GR 163273,
    GR 123262, GR 115282, GR 120253
Translation: rocky hollow; hill of the moss; file
    hill; Finlay's hill; hill of the barns
Pronunciation: tow kraykach; towm a
    choanyeech; kaarn aya; byn yoony; mam sool
Access Point: Glen Affric, GR 215242
Distance/ascent: 23mls/7600ft; 37km/2316m
Approx Time: 10-16 hours

🚶 From the car park near the head of Loch Affric
a path runs north into Gleann nam Fiadh. As it
turns west into the glen another path leaves the
riverside and climbs NW over the Bealach Toll
Easa. Toll Creagach can easily be climbed from
the summit of this pass, and so can Tom
a'Choinich. From here continue west over the
undulating, and in places rough, ridge. Cross
the deep notch of the Garbh-bhealach and
continue past the needles of Stob Coire
Dhomhnuill (easily turned on the left), round
the head of Coire Dhomhain to Creag na h-Eige
and then to the great dome of Carn Eige itself.
From the summit head north to Beinn
Fhionnlaidh, a long pull involves a 1000ft/305m
drop and a pull up the other side. Return
towards Carn Eige but the climb back to the
summit can be avoided by a traverse up the
west slopes to the pass between Carn Eige and
Mam Sodhail. Continue to the summit cairn, a
massive structure built round the OS pillar.

An Riabhachan from the slopes of Sgurr na Lapaich

Return to Glen Affric via the ridge which runs
SE over Mullach Cadha Rainich and Sgurr na
Lapaich avoiding the latter's craggy eastern
cliffs.

Forestry Commission. Tel: 01463-232811.

CARN NAN GOBHAR, 3255FT/992M
SGURR NA LAPAICH, 3772FT/1150M
AN RIABHACHAN, 3704FT/1129M
AN SOCACH, 3507FT/1069M

Map: OS Sheet 25: GR 182344, GR 161351,
GR 134345, GR 100333
Translation: hill of the goats; peak of the bog; the
brindled, greyish one; the snout
*Pronunciation: kaarn nan gower; skoor na
lahpeech; an reeavachan; an sochkach*
Access Point: Mullardoch Dam, GR 222310
Distance/ascent: 19mls/6200ft; 30km/1890m
Approx Time: 9-13 hours

Follow the stalkers' path up the east bank of
the Allt Mullardoch and into Coire an t-Sith.
Continue to climb north up the steep slopes of
Creag Dhubh where the ridge is reached.
Follow the ridge WSW to the summit of Carn
nan Gobhar. Follow the broad ridge NW over a
wide grassy saddle beyond which a steeper rib
leads to the summit of Sgurr na Lapaich. Leave
the summit by the SW shoulder and descend
steeply to a col, the Bealach Toll an Lochain.

Sgurr na Ruaidhe in the Strathfarrar Hills

Follow the rim of An Riabhachan's NE corrie to
the NE top and then across to the summit itself.
From the summit cross to the SW top and here
the main ridge turns NW towards the west top
where a twist in the ridge leads down to another
bealach below An Socach. Climb easily to the
broad summit. To return to Glen Cannich
follow the south ridge which then sweeps round
to the SE and the long indistinct path alongside
Loch Mullardoch.

🦌 Balmore and Cozac Estate Keeper. Tel: 01463-
232339.

SGURR FHUAR-THUILL, **3441FT/1049M**
SGURR A'CHOIRE GHLAIS, **3553FT/1083M**
CARN NAN GHOBHAR, **3255FT/992M**
SGURR NA RUAIDHE, **3258FT/993M**

Map: OS Sheet 25: GR 235437, GR 259430,
   GR 273439, GR 289426
Translation: peak of the cold hollow; peak of the
   greenish-grey corrie; hill of the goats; peak of
   redness
Pronunciation: skoor oar hil; skoor a
   choraghlash; kaarn nan gower; skoor na rooy
Access Point: Braulen Lodge, GR 237387
Distance/ascent: 14mls/5000ft; 22km/1524m
Approx Time: 6-10 hours

※ Access to Glen Strathfarrar is via a locked gate at Struy. Permission and a key for the lock can be obtained by telephoning 01463-761260, the cottage beside the gate. A stalkers' path climbs north into the corrie of Loch Toll a'Mhuic and on up the steep back wall of the corrie to finish just below the crest of Sgurr na Fearstaig. From here continue east to Sgurr Fhur-thuill. The crest of the ridge is broad so follow the rim east, over the undulation of Creag Ghorm a'Bhealaich and down to the narrow saddle before Sgurr a'Choire Ghlais. Return to the main crest and descend to a saddle at the foot of Carn nan Ghobhar, from where an easy 400ft/122m climb leads to the stony summit. Continue east, then SE, and down into the Bealach nam Bogan then slopes to Sgurr na Ruaidhe.

🦌 Broulin Estate. Tel: 01463-761260.

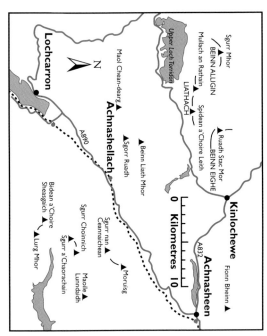

Suggested Base Achnasheen or Torridon
Accommodation Hotels, guest houses and b/b at
  Achnasheen, Strathcarron,
  Torridon. Youth Hostels at
  Torridon. Private hostel at
  Craig, Achnashellach.
Public Transport Rail: Inverness to Kyle of
  Lochalsh. Stations at
  Achnasheen, Achnashellach and
  Strathcarron. Buses: Inverness
  to Poolewe for Achnasheen and
  Kinlochewe , for onward post
  bus service. Post buses:
  Achnasheen to Laide for
  Kinlochewe; Kinlochewe to
  Diabaig for Torridon.

MORUISG, 3045FT/928M
SGURR NAN CEANNAICHEAN, 3002FT/915M

Map: OS Sheet 25: GR 101499, GR 087481
Translation: big water; peak of the pedlars
Pronunciation: moarishk; skoor nan kyaneechan
Access Point: Glen Carron, GR 081521
Distance/ascent: 8mls/3500ft; 13km/1067m
Approx Time: 4-6 hours

⚲ Leave the A890 Glen Carron road at a car park about three-quarters of a mile west of the outflow of Loch Sgamhain. Cross the footbridge over the river and take a stalkers' path which runs up the east bank of the Alltan na Feola. After about 2.5km leave the burn and climb east up grassy slopes. Continue until you reach the broad crest. Continue on the crest NE to the summit. Return and follow the broad ridge south over a subsidiary top and then descend more steeply SW to an obvious col. Climb west to reach the flat summit of Sgurr nan Ceanaichean. The summit cairn overlooks the east corrie. Retrace your steps down the NE ridge then bear north down a steep ridge back to the Alltan na Feola.

🦌 Glen Carron Estate. Tel: 01520-766275.

MAOILE LUNNDAIDH, 3304FT/1007M
SGURR A'CHAORACHAIN, 3455FT/1053M
SGURR CHOINNICH, 3277FT/999M

Map: OS Sheet 25: GR 135458, GR 087447,
  GR 076446
Translation: bare hill of the wet place; peak of the little field of the berries; moss peak
Pronunciation: moela loondy; skoor a choerachan; skoor choanyeech
Access Point: Craig, GR 038493
Distance/ascent: 20mls/5500ft; 32km/1676m
Approx Time: 8-12 hours

⚲ Cross the railway and follow the Forestry Commission road, first parallel to the railway, then up through the forest to the locked gate at the top edge of the forest. Beyond the gate a

Sgurr Choinnich and Sgurr a'Chaorachain

path runs below the steep east face of Sgurr
nan Ceanaichean and alongside the Allt
a'Chonais. Continue on the track until it turns
east towards distant Strathconon. Hereabouts a
footbridge crosses the river and another track
runs SW up and over the Bealach Bearnais.
Follow this track a good distance up towards
the bealach and then heading back east by way
of the west ridge of Sgurr Choinnich. From the
summit continue east across the flat summit and
then down to the bealach before the long pull to
Sgurr a'Chaorachain. Continue past the
summit on broad slopes in an ESE direction
towards Bidean an Eoin Deirg and from the
bealach just before that summit, drop down
steep slopes in a NE direction to reach the small
lochan which lies at the foot of the west ridge of
Carn nam Fiaclan. Ascend this ridge on to a
broad tableland, cross the bealach at the head
of Fuar-tholl Mor and cross a broad and
featureless plateau in a NE direction to the
large cairn on the summit of Maoile Lunndaidh.
Descend north along the east rim of the Fuar-
tholl Mor and down into Glean Fhiodhaig. A
path will take you west back to the starting
point.
🦌 Achnashellach Estate. Tel: 01520-766266.

BIDEIN A'CHOIRE SHEASGAICH, 3100FT/945M
LURG MHOR, 3235FT/986M

Map: OS Sheet 25: GR 049413, GR 165405
Translation: peak of the corrie of the milkless
  cattle; big ridge stretching into the plain
Pronunciation: beetyan a chora haysgeech;
  loorak voar
Access Point: Craig, GR 038493
Distance/ascent: 18mls/5200ft; 29km/1585m
Approx Time: 8-12 hours

🚶 From the footbridge over the Allt a'Chonais
follow the footpath to the summit of the Bealach
Bernais. From the boggy summit leave the path
and climb the NE ridge of Beinn Tharsuinn
crossing several undulations before reaching
the summit. Descend SW to a small lochan and
then WSW to an obvious col between the
summit and the west top. From here drop down
steep slopes for a considerable distance to reach
the floor of the Bealach an Sgoltaidh. Steep and
craggy flanks guard Bidein a'Choire Sheasgaich
but an easier route can be found by traversing
slightly to the right and so avoiding the steepest
of the crags. A steep path zig-zags its way up
and you will top out beside a small lochan.
Continue south to the pointed summit of
Sheasgaich. From the summit descend south,
then SE and follow the broad ridge to Lurg
Mhor. To return you have to retrace your steps
all the way to the Bealach Bearnais and the Allt
a'Chonais.

🦌 Achnashellach Estate. Tel: 01520-766266.

BEINN LIATH MHOR, 3035FT/925M
SGORR RUADH, 3150FT/960M

Map: OS Sheet 25: GR 964520, GR 959504
Translation: big grey hill; red peak
Pronunciation: byn leea voar; skoor rooa
Access Point: Achnashellach, GR 002485
Distance/ascent: 9mls/3750ft; 14km/1143m
Approx Time: 5-8 hours

⚮ Take the path from Achnashellach station through the pines above the River Lair. Climb above the forest on the path to a heathery hillside beneath the craggy terminal of Beinn Liath Mhor. Here the path separates, with one path running NW into Coire Lair and the other running NE into the Easan Dorcha. Take the latter for a short distance to its highest point, and then take the steep and unrelenting heather slopes of Beinn Liath Mhor. Climb to its east top and follow the stony quartzite ridge WNW to the summit. Continue on the ridge, narrow in places and descend to the Bealach Coire Lair, taking care as there are some crags to bypass and a prominent knoll either to cross, or circumnavigate. From the bealach climb south on to the NW ridge of Sgurr Ruadh and follow this ridge SE to the steep and prominent summit. The descent SE is via the Bealach Mhoir and wide open slopes back to the River Lair.

🦌 Achnashellach Estate. Tel: 01520-766266.

MAOL CHEAN-DEARG, 3061FT/933M

Map: OS Sheet 25: GR 924498
Translation: bald red head
Pronunciation: moel chan jerrack
Access Point: Coulags, GR 962451
Distance/ascent: 8mls/3000ft; 13km/914m
Approx Time: 3-5 hours

⚮ From Coulags follow the path on the east side of Fionn-abhainn. Cross the bridge to the west side after 2.5km or so and continue past the bothy to the Clach nan Con-fionn. Shortly after this take the path which bears off west and climb to the col between Maol Chean-dearg and Meall nan Ceapairean. Turn NW here and climb the broad ridge to the summit.

🦌 Achnashellach Estate. Tel: 01520-766266.

FIONN BHEINN, 3061FT/933M

Map: OS Sheets 20 and 25: GR 147621
Translation: pale coloured hill

Beinn Alligin

Pronunciation: fyoon vyn
Access Point: Achnasheen, GR 158585
Distance/ascent: 4mls/3000ft; 6km/914m
Approx Time: 3-5 hours

🐾 Follow the Allt Achadh na Sine from
   Achnasheen and keep to its NE bank. Follow
   the burn high up into a corrie west of Creagan
   nan Laogh and climb grassy slopes north to the
   ridge. Follow the ridge west to the summit.
🐎 Lochrosque Estate. Tel: 01445-720266.

BEINN ALLIGIN, 3232FT/985M

Map: OS Sheets 19 and 24: GR 866613
Translation: jewelled hill
Pronunciation: byn alligin
Access Point: Coire Mhic Nobuil bridge car park,
   GR 869576
Distance/ascent: 6mls/3800ft; 10km/1158m
Approx Time: 4-6 hours

🐾 Cross the road and take the path which crosses
   the moorland towards Coir' nan Laogh of Tom
   na Gruagaich. Climb to the head of the corrie
   and ascend Tom na Gruagaich itself. Descend
   north down a rocky ridge to a col beyond which
   the ridge becomes broader. Climb NNE over a
   knoll, drop a little height to a bealach and then
   climb NE to Sgurr Mhor, the summit of Beinn

Alligin. From here descend steeply ENE then east down a narrow ridge to a col. Follow the well-marked path over the Horns of Alligin, using hands as well as feet in places. From the third 'Horn' continue the descent SE to the moorland and the track in Coire Mhic Nobuil is joined.

🦌 National Trust for Scotland. No restrictions.

BEINN EIGHE (RUADH-STAC MOR), 3314FT/1010M

Map: OS Sheets 19 and 25: GR 951611
Translation: file hill, (big red peak)
Pronunciation: byn ay
Access Point: Car park on A896, GR 958568
Distance/ascent: 10mls/3200ft; 16km/975m
Approx Time: 4-6 hours

🐾 Leave the car park and follow the broad track which leads up Coire Dubh Mor. At GR 934594 take another path which runs north round the prow of Sail Mor and traverses the hillside before climbing up into Coire Mhic Fhearchair. Cross the outflow of the loch and follow the east side of the loch before climbing screes and rough slopes SE to reach the ridge which leads to the summit, Ruadh-stac Mor. The traverse of Beinn Eighe can be continued to take in Coinneach Mhor, Spidean Coire nan Clach and along the main ridge to Sgurr Ban and Sgurr nan Fhir Duibhe.

🦌 Scottish Natural Heritage. No restrictions.

LIATHACH, SPIDEAN A'CHOIRE LEITH, 3458FT/1054M
MULLACH AN RATHAIN, 3356FT/1023M

Map: O S Sheet 25: GR 929580, GR 912577
Translation: grey one, peak of the grey corrie; summit of the row of pinnacles
Pronunciation: leeahach, speetyan a chora lay; moolach an raahan
Access Point: A896, half mile east of Glen Cottage, GR 936566
Distance/ascent: 7mls/4300ft; 11km/1311m
Approx Time: 5-8 hours

Liathach

🐾 Leave the road just east of Glen Cottage and
climb steeply up the craggy hillside into the Toll
a'Meitheach. Higher up the corrie climb up
rightwards, NE, over steep ground to the col on
the main ridge. Follow the ridge NW then west
over two small tops to the cone of Spidean
a'Choire Leith. Descend SW to a short and
level grassy section. Continue over, or around
the pinnacles of Am Fasarinen. A path avoids
the difficulties on the south side. Beyond the
pinnacles it is an easy stroll on to Mullach an
Rathain. From the summit the most interesting
descent back to Glen Torridon is via the SW
ridge.
🦌 National Trust for Scotland. No restrictions.

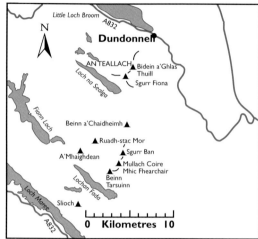

Suggested Base	Kinlochewe or Dundonnell
Accommodation	Hotels, b/b in Kinlochewe, Poolewe, Dundonnell. Hostel at Sail Mhor, Dundonnell. Caravan site at Kinlochewe. Camping/caravan site at Gairloch.
Public Transport	Rail: Inverness to Kyle of Lochalsh, with stations at Garve and Achnasheen for onward bus services. Buses: Inverness to Poolewe for Kinlochewe. Inverness to Braemore and Gairloch for Dundonnell.

SLIOCH, 3215FT/980M

Map: OS Sheet 19: GR 005688
Translation: from the Gaelic sleagh, a spear
Pronunciation: slee-och
Access Point: Incheril, Kinlochewe, GR 038624
Distance/ascent: 12mls/3500ft; 19km/1067m
Approx Time: 6-9 hours

⚕ From the car park at Incheril follow the path which runs along the north bank of the Kinlochewe River. After 5km cross the Abhainn an Fhasaigh by a footbridge and turn right on the path which runs up Gleann Bianasdail. After 1km branch left on the well worn path which climbs north towards Slioch's SE corrie, Coire Tuill Bhain. Continue to gain the SE ridge and climb to the trig point summit. From here cross the slight depression which leads to the north top which is the same height. Follow the narrowing ridge to Sgurr an Tuill Bhain and descend steep slopes south back into the corrie.

⚔ Kinlochewe Estate. Tel: 01445-760247.

RUADH STAC MOR, 3012FT/918M
A'MHAIGHDEAN, 3173FT/967M

Map: OS Sheet 19: GR 018756, GR 008749
Translation: big red peak; the maiden
Pronunciation: roo-a stak more; ah-vtyin
Access Point: Poolewe, GR 856854
Distance/ascent: 25mls/3900ft; 40km/1189m
Approx Time: 10-14 hours

⚕ A private road leaves Poolewe and runs along the east side of the River Ewe to Inveran and Kernsary. (Tel: 01445-781337 for permission and key to drive as far as Kernsary.) From Kernsary go east then SE through forest to reach the path on the north bank of the Allt na Creige. This path is indistinct in places but soon descends to pass Loch an Doire Chrionaich. Continue south to cross Strathan Buidhe then continue to SE end of Fionn Loch. Cross the causeway between Fionn Loch and Dubh Loch and follow stalkers' path to Carnmore. Continue east, cross the Allt Bruthach an Easain and traverse SE across the hillside to reach the NW ridge of A'Mhaighdean. Follow the craggy ridge to the summit. From here descend NE to the grassy col below Ruadh Stac Mor. Climb the sandstone crags in a northerly direction to the summit trig point. Return to the col and take the stalkers'

path to Carnmore and the return journey to
Poolewe.
🦌 Ardlair/Fisherfield/Letterewe. Tel: 01445-781215.

BEINN A'CHLAIDHEIMH, 3000FT/914M
SGURR BAN, 3245FT/989M
MULLACH COIRE MHIC FHEARCHAIR, 3343FT/1019M
BEINN TARSUINN, 3071FT/936M

Map: OS Sheet 19: GR 061775, GR 055745,
  GR 052735, GR 039727
Translation: hill of the sword; light-coloured peak;
  summit of the corrie of Farquhar's son;
  transverse hill
Pronunciation: byn a'shleev; skoor bawn;
  moolach mora veechk erachar; byn tarshin
Access Point: Shenavall, GR 066810
Distance/ascent: 13mls/5800ft; 21km/1768m
Approx Time: 8-12 hours

🦌 From the bothy at Shenavall (GR 066810) cross
the Abhainn Strath na Sealga. (Take care; the
crossing of this river when in spate is not
advisable and there is no bridge.) Climb the
steep heather-covered slopes of Beinn
a'Chlaidheimh to the SW. The slope becomes
steeper as you reach the summit ridge and the
final pull is up the ridge just east of the summit.
Descend to the south on long scree slopes
towards Loch a'Bhrisidh and follow the corrie
rim to the summit of Sgurr Ban over acres of
white quartzite scree. Continue to another scree
filled col just south of Sgurr Ban where another
steep climb takes you to the summit of Mullach
Coire Mhic Fhearchair. Continue south to a
prominent knob where the mountain's south
ridge suddenly turns west to Beinn Tarsuinn.
This can be turned by easy slopes to the east
and south. Continue over rocky platforms to
the summit of Beinn Tarsuinn. To return to
Shenavall take a line across the north slopes to
reach the stalkers' path in Gleann na Muice.
🦌 Ardlair/Fisherfield/Letterewe. Tel: 01445-781215.

AN TEALLACH, SGURR FIONA, 3474FT/1059M
BIDEIN A'GHLAS THUILL, 3484FT/1062M

Map: OS Sheet 19: GR 064837, GR 069844
Translation: the forge, peak of wine; peak of the
   greenish-grey hollow
Pronunciation: an tyalach, skoor fee-ana;
   beetyan a ghlas hil
Access Point: Dundonnell, GR 090880
Distance/ascent: 13 mls/5200ft; 21km/1585m
Approx Time: 6-10 hours

Leave the A832 road about 500 metres SE of
the hotel and follow the path which zig-zags up
the steep shoulder of Meall Garbh. The path
disappears around the 750-metres contour so
follow the broad stony ridge south over a
prominent knoll to another knoll from where a
short ascent ESE takes you to an unnamed top
at the edge of Glas Tholl. Descend south to a
col and then follow the easy ridge to the summit
of Bidein a'Ghlas Thuill. Descend SSW to a col
and then climb the steep and rocky ridge to the
summit of Sgurr Fiona. For a more interesting
descent follow the line of the SE ridge past (or
over if you don't mind an exposed scramble)
the imposing Lord Berkeley's Seat and the
Corrag Bhuidhe pinnacles to Sail Liath.
Continue SE on the ridge to reach the cairned
path which runs from Shenavall to Dundonnell.
Eilean Darach Estate. Tel: 01854-633203.
Dundonnell Estate. Tel: 01854-633219.

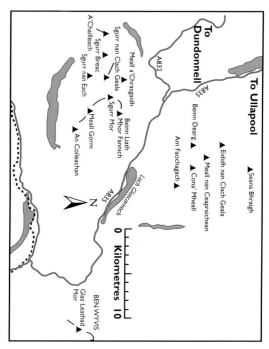

Suggested Base Garve or Ullapool
Accommodation Hotels, guest houses and b/b at
Garve, Ullapool, Oykel Bridge
and Aultguish. Youth Hostel at
Ullapool. Camping/caravan sites
at Ullapool and Garve.
Public Transport Rail: Inverness to Kyle of
Lochalsh. Station at Garve for
onward bus services. Buses:
Inverness to Gairloch for
Garve, Garbat, Aultguish,
Dirrie More and Braemore.
Inverness to Ullapool for Garve,
Garbat, Aultguish, Dirrie More
and Inverlael. Lairg to

Lochinver for Oykel Bridge (for
Strath Mulzie).

AN COILEACHAN, 3028FT/923M
MEALL GORM, 3113FT/949M
SGURR MOR, 3645FT/1111M
BEINN LIATH MHOR FANNAICH, 3130FT/954M
MEALL A'CHRASGAIDH, 3064FT/934M
SGURR NAN CLACH GEALA, 3586FT/1093M
SGURR NAN EACH, 3028FT/923M

Map: OS Sheet: 20: GR 241680, GR 221696,
   GR 203718, GR 219724, GR 184733,
   GR 184715, GR 184697
Translation: the little cock; blue hill; big peak; big
   grey hill of Fannich; hill of the crossing; peak
   of the white stones; peak of the horses
Pronunciation: an kilyachan; myowl gorram;
   skoor more; byn leea voar fannich; myowl a
   chraskee; skoor nan klach gyala; skoor nan
   yach
Access Point: Fannich Lodge, GR 218660
Distance/ascent: 15mls/6500ft; 24km/1981m
Approx Time: 8-12 hours

அ Permission can be gained to drive from Grudie
   bridge to Fannich Lodge, a distance of seven
   miles (11.2km). Telephone the keeper at
   Fannich Lodge on 01997-414227. From Fannich
   Lodge climb the slopes of An Coileachan from
   where a broad ridge stretches in a NW
   direction to Meall Gorm where two tops appear
   as little more than the high spots on a broad
   and featureless ridge. The true summit is the
   one with a wind-break shelter built near it.
   Continue over the long pull to Meall nam
   Peithirean and onwards towards Sgurr Mor.
   Just before the final rise to the summit of Sgurr
   Mor, however, a ridge breaks off east to the
   summit of Beinn Liath Mhor Fannaich. Return
   to Sgurr Mor and continue NW to Carn na
   Chriche and Meall a'Chrasgaidh. Leave the
   summit in a southerly direction, cross the
   saddle of Am Biachdiach and climb the steep
   and rocky NNE ridge of Sgurr nan Clach
   Geala. Continue easily south to Sgurr nan Each

and then south and SE to the track beside Loch
Fannich.

🦌 Eastern Munros — Fannich Estate. Tel: 01997-
414227. Western Munros — Fannich Estate.
Tel: 01343-820213.

A'CHAILLEACH, 3277FT/999M
SGURR BREAC, 3281FT/1000M

Map: OS Sheets 19 and 20: GR 136714,
   GR 158711
Translation: the old woman; specked peak
Pronunciation: a chalyach; skoor brechk
Access Point: A832 near Loch a'Bhraoin,
   GR 161761
Distance/ascent: 10mls/3750ft; 16km/1143m
Approx Time: 5-8 hours

🚶 Take the private road to Loch a'Bhraoin. Cross
its outlet and continue on the stalkers' path
beside the Allt Breabaig in a southerly direction
as far as the high bealach which leads over to
Loch Fannich. From the pass climb the east
ridge of Sgurr Breac. Continue by traversing
Toman Coinich and descending to the col below
its west slopes. Follow the rim of the corrie Toll
an Lochain to its junction with the Sron na
Goibhre spur then continue SW along a gently
rising ridge to the summit of A'Chailleach.

🦌 Fannich Estate. Tel: 01343-820213.

BEN WYVIS, GLAS LEATHAD MOR, 3432FT/1046M

Map: OS Sheet 20: GR 463684
Translation: from the Gaelic fuathas — possibly
   hill of terror, big greenish grey slope
Pronunciation: byn wivis, glas lehat moar
Access Point: Garbat, GR 412678
Distance/ascent: 14mls/4300ft; 22km/1311m
Approx Time: 6-10 hours

🚶 Take the muddy track which runs alongside the
Allt a'Bhealaich Mhoir. Continue past the
forestry plantation and turn uphill to climb the
steep slopes of An Cabar. From the top the
summit lies just over a mile in a NE direction

over a rolling mossy ridge.

🦌 Mountgarret Estate. Tel: 01349-862144.

AM FAOCHAGACH, 3130FT/954M

Map: OS Sheet 20: GR 304794
Translation: place of the shells
Pronunciation: am foechakach
Access Point: A835 NW end of Loch Glascarnoch,
  GR 276743
Distance/ascent: 9mls/2300ft; 14km/701m
Approx Time: 4-6 hours

🚶 Start at the bridge over the Abhainnan an
  Torrain Dubh. Cross the moorland in an
  easterly direction passing between Loch
  Glascarnoch and Loch a'Gharbhrain. The
  crossing of the Abhainn a'Gharbhrain will
  entail wading to a greater or lesser degree
  depending on the weather conditions. Once
  across the river turn NE and climb the steep
  heather slopes to reach the main ridge just
  south of the summit. From there the going is
  easy along a broad and obvious ridge.
🦌 Braemore Estate. Tel: 01854-655222.

BEINN DEARG, 3556FT/1084M
CONA'MHEALL, 3215FT/980M
MEALL NAN CEAPRAICHEAN, 3205FT/977M
EIDIDH NAN CLACH GEALA, 3045FT/928M

Map: OS Sheet 20: GR 259812, GR 275816,
  GR 257826, GR 257843
Translation: red hill; hill of the joining; possibly
  from ceap, meaning a rounded hilltop; web of
  the white stones
*Pronunciation: byn dyerak; konival; myowl nan
  kyapreechan; aydyee nan klach gyala*
Access Point: Inverlael, GR 182853
Distance/ascent: 15mls/5000ft; 24km/1524m
Approx Time: 7-11 hours

🚶 Take the private road through the forest into
  Gleann na Squaib. Follow the stalkers' path up
  the glen to the broad saddle at its head. From
  the saddle go south by a massive drystone dyke

and follow it up Beinn Dearg's north ridge.
Where the dyke turns west go through a gap
and cross the bald summit dome in a SSW
direction to the cairn. Return to the saddle and
climb the easy angled ridge to the east to
Cona'Mheall. Return to the saddle and climb
the broad SE ridge of Meall nan Ceapraichean.
Continue NE along a broad stony ridge to
Ceann Garbh, descend NE down rocky and
craggy slopes to another col at the foot of
Eididh nan Clach Geala's SE ridge. Climb the
easy grassy ridge to the top where the NW cairn
is the summit. Descend west down grassy slopes
for a short distance then go SW into the corrie
west of Lochan na Chnapaich where a path
leads downhill to the main path in Gleann na
Squaib.

🦌 Inverlael Estate. Tel: 01854-655262.

SEANA BHRAIGH, 3041FT/927M

Map: OS Sheet 20: GR 281879
Translation: old upper part
Pronunciation: shena vry
Access Point: Inverlael, GR 182853
Distance/ascent: 16mls/3700ft; 26km/1128m
Approx Time: 7-10 hours

🐾 From Inverlael follow the forest track as far as
Glensquaib. Continue by the stalkers' track
which leads out of the forest and on to the
Druim na Saobhaidhe ridge. From this ridge
cross the wide corrie of Gleann a'Mhadaidh
and round a spur of hills above to continue up
Coire an Lochain Sgeirich. Continue across
boggy terrain towards Loch a'Chadha Dheirg
from where a northerly direction will take you
to the easy slopes to the SW top. From there
follow the cliff edge to the summit of Seana
Bhraigh.

🦌 Inverlael Estate. Tel: 01854-655262.

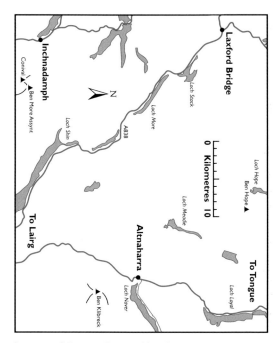

Suggested Base	Lairg, Altnaharra or Inchnadamph
Accommodation	Hotels at Altnaharra, Crask Inn, Tongue, Lairg and Inchnadamph. Youth Hostels at Durness and Tongue. Camping/caravan sites at Lairg and Tongue.
Public Transport	Rail: Inverness to Wick and Thurso. Station at Lairg for onward post bus. Buses: Inverness to Wick and Thurso for Bonar Bridge; Inverness to Dornoch for Bonar Bridge; Bonar Bridge to Lairg; Lairg to Lochinver for Inchnadamph;

Thurso to Tongue. Post buses:
Lairg to Talmine for Crask Inn
(Klibreck). Altnaharra to
Portnacon and Rispond for
Atnacallich.

BEN MORE ASSYNT, 3274FT/998M
CONIVAL, 3238FT/987M

Map: OS Sheet 15: GR 318201, GR 303199
Translation: big hill of Assynt; hill of joining
Pronunciation: byn moar assint; konival
Access Point: Inchnadamph, GR 251216
Distance/ascent: 11mls/3700ft; 18km/1128m
Approx Time: 4-7 hours

🐾 Take the farm track, just north of the
Inchnadamph Hotel, which runs alongside the
River Traligill. Follow the path to the Traligill
Caves, but stay on the NE bank. Opposite the
caves leave the track and take to the slopes on
the SW face of Beinn an Fhurain. Aim for the
obvious col between Beinn an Fhurain and
Conival. From the col the final slopes lead to a
level ridge and the summit. Continue east for a
mile along the rough ridge of scree and crag to
the summit of Ben More Assynt. The summit
cairn is on the north top.
🦌 Inchnadamph Estate. Tel: 01571-822221.

BEN KLIBRECK, 3153FT/961M

Map: OS Sheet 16: GR 585299
Translation: hill of the speckled cliff
Pronunciation: byn kleebreck
Access Point: A836 Lairg/Tongue road, GR
545303
Distance/ascent: 7 mls/2600ft; 11km/792m
Approx Time: 4-6 hours

🐾 Cross the river (no footbridge) and go east across
the moorland towards Loch nan Uan. From the
north end of the loch go SE up steep grassy
slopes to the main ridge. Follow the easy ridge to
a bouldery slope which leads to the summit.
🦌 Altnaharra Estate. Tel: 01549-411220.

BEN HOPE, 3041FT/927M

Map: OS Sheet 9: GR 477502
Translation: hill of the bay
Pronunciation: byn hope
Access Point: Alltnacaillich, GR 459456
Distance/ascent: 4mls/3000ft; 6km/914m
Approx Time: 2-4 hours

𝕸 From the farm at Alltnacaillich go north for a mile and leave the road by a sheep shed. Follow the stream and head NE to make for an obvious break in the crags which takes you on to a wide terrace above the escarpment. Turn north and follow the cliff edge which buttresses the mountain's summit.

𝕬 Eriboll Estate. Tel: 01549-411248.

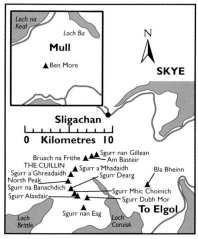

Suggested Base	Glen Brittle (Skye)
Accommodation	Hotels, guest houses and b/b at Broadford, Portree, Sligachan and Carbost. Youth Hostels at Broadford and Glen Brittle. Camp site at Glen Brittle.
Public Transport	Rail: Inverness to Kyle of Lochalsh and Glasgow to Mallaig for ongoing ferries and bus services. Inverness to Kyle of Lochalsh for toll bridge. Buses: Glasgow and Fort William to Uig. Edinburgh and Perth to Portree. Inverness to Portree. Portree to Fiskavaig for Sligachan and Carbost (nearest village to Glen Brittle). Armadale to Kyleakin for Broadford. Post bus: Broadford to Elgol for Torrin and Loch Slapin.

Suggested Base	Tobermory (Mull)
Accommodation	Hotels, guest houses and b/b at Tombermory. Youth Hostel.
Public Transport	Ferry: Oban to Craignure. Buses: Craignure to Tobermory.

BLA BHEINN (BLAVEN), 3045FT/928M

Map: OS Sheet 32: GR 530217
Translation: possibly blue hill, or possibly warm hill
Pronunciation: blaavin
Access Point: Head of Loch Slapin, GR 561218
Distance/ascent: 4mls/3100ft; 6km/945m
Approx Time: 2-5 hours

🐾 Leave the Elgol Road at the Allt na Dunaiche just south of the head of Loch Slapin on its west side. Take the path that runs alongside the north bank of the stream through a wooded gorge, and then more steeply into Coire Uaigneich. Here the path becomes indistinct in places, but turns NNW up a steep slope just right of an obvious gully and soon reaches on to a distinct shoulder. Once this shoulder abuts on to the main ridge follow it in a WSW direction, following the rim of the ridge. As you climb closer to the summit dome there are one or two rocky obstacles to be scrambled over before more scree slopes lead to the summit.

🦌 Strathaird Estate. Tel: 01471-866232.

SGURR DUBH MOR, 3097FT/944M
SGURR NAN EAG, 3037FT/924M

Map: OS Sheet 32: GR 457205, GR 457195
Translation: big black peak; peak of the notches
Pronunciation: skoor doo moar; skoor nan ayg
Access Point: Glen Brittle House, GR 413208
Distance/ascent: 9mls/3900ft; 14km/1189m
Approx Time: 4-6 hours

🐾 From the camp site in Glen Brittle follow the track towards Coire Lagan but after half a mile or so leave the path and cross the moorland in an ESE direction towards Sron na Ciche. Make for the edge of Coir' a'Ghrunnda by contouring around the foot of Sron na Ciche, and then climb into the corrie to reach the lochan. From the lochan climb easy slopes which lead to an obvious col on the main ridge between Sgurr Dubh na Da Bheinn and Sgurr Thearlaich. Climb easy slopes to Sgurr Dubh na Da Bheinn and from there follow the ridge east to Sgurr Dubh Mor. Return to Sgurr Dubh na Da Bheinn and descend south along the main ridge, traversing below the steep-sided Caisteal a'Garbh-choire on either its west or east side. Continue along the main ridge to Sgurr nan Eag.

🦌 No restrictions.

SGURR ALASDAIR, 3258FT/993M
SGURR MHIC CHOINNICH, 3110FT/948M
INACCESSIBLE PINNACLE, 3235FT/986M

Map: OS Sheet 32: GR 449208, GR 450210, GR 444215
Translation: Alexander's Peak (named after Sheriff Alexander Nicolson who made the first ascent in 1873), MacKenzie's Peak (named after John MacKenzie the first Skye guide), the Innaccessible Pinnacle is affectionately known as the 'Inn Pin'.
Pronunciation: skoor alastar; skoor veechk chunyeech
Access Point: Glen Brittle, GR 413208
Distance/ascent: 9mls/5500ft; 14km/1676m
Approx Time: 6-8 hours

🏔 Sgurr Alasdair by way of the Sron na Ciche above Coir' a'Ghrunnda. This involves a section between Sgurr Sgumain and Sgurr Alasdair which includes some climbing of a difficult standard, but that can be avoided by going a few yards towards the Coir' a'Ghrunnda side of the ridge where a short chimney offers an easier scramble back to the main ridge and to the summit. From here descend to the gap between Alasdair and Sgurr Thearlaich, and scramble up the latter's southern rib to the summit. Take care on the

Peaks above Coire Laggan — Sgurr Alasdair and Sgurr Mhic Choinnich

descent to the gap before Sgurr Mhic Choinnich — there is much loose rock and the route is not entirely obvious. From here move up a little and then traverse round the west face by Collie's Ledge (moderate difficulty — rock climbing). A much more direct route for climbers takes the obvious corner of King's Chimney (difficult) on the south side. Walkers who don't wish to climb are best descending to Coire Lagan by the Great Stone Chute between Sgurr Alasdair and Sgurr Thearlaich, regaining the ridge by the An Stac screes. From the summit of Sgurr Mhic Choinnich descend NNE to the col above the An Stac screes. It will be necessary to drop down a little to reach a cairned path in the scree which leads up below the west edge of An Stac's tower. Staying close to the base of its wall climb to easier ground. Continue on the main ridge and climb the Inaccessible Pinnacle by its east ridge (moderate difficulty — rock climbing). On the tiny summit a convenient boulder provides an anchor for a 60 foot/18m abseil off the west side of the pinnacle. Descend to Glen Brittle by Sgurr Dearg's west ridge.

🦌 No restrictions.

Sgurr na Banachdich, 3166ft/965m
Sgurr a'Chreadaidh, 3192ft/973m
Sgurr a'Mhadaidh, 3012ft/918m

Map: OS Sheet 32: GR 440225, GR 445232,
   GR 446235
Translation: possibly smallpox peak; peak of
   torment; peak of the fox
Pronunciation: skoor na banachteech; skoor a
   ghraytee; skoor a vaady
Access Point: Glen Brittle, GR 413208
Distance/ascent: 9mls/4400ft; 14km/1341m
Approx Time: 4-6 hours

🐾 Take the path above the Eas Mor waterfalls to
the upper basin of Coire na Banachdich. From
here a cairned route takes a devious line
beneath the crags of Sgurr Dearg eventually
turning left to reach screes which lead to a gap
in the ridge north of Sgurr Dearg. To the north,
across the Bealach Coire na Banachdich, steep
rock and screes lead to Sron Bhuidhe, then two
more 'tops' before the final pull to Sgurr na
Banachdich. From the summit a short dip leads
to the foot of Sgurr Thormaid. This is climbed
by scrambling over large blocks and boulders.
From the summit continue to the NE avoiding
the 'three teeth' by traversing easy angled slabs
on their left. Follow the short narrow aràte
which leads to a 400-foot/120m scramble on
good holds to the south top of Sgurr
a'Ghreadaidh. Follow the very narrow ridge
crest to the summit. Continue on the narrow
ridge down into the gap known as the Eag
Dubh. This is followed by another descent to a
second gap, the An Dorus. From here scramble
to the SW summit of Sgurr a'Mhadaidh, the
only 'top' which is given Munro status. Follow
the ridge NW which runs out to Sgurr Thuilm
and drop down into Coire an Durus from the
obvious col, returning to Glen Brittle.
🦌 No restrictions.

SGURR NAN GILLEAN, 3166FT/965M
AM BASTEIR, 3068FT/935M
BRUACH NA FRITHE, 3143FT/958M

Map: OS Sheet 32: GR 472253, GR 465253,
   GR 461252
Translation: peak of the young men; meaning
   obscure; slope of the deer forest
Pronunciation: skoor nan geelyan; am baastyer;
   brooach na freea
Access Point: Sligachan, GR 486298
Distance/ascent: 9mls/3800ft; 14km/1158m
Approx Time: 4-7 hours

A well-maintained footpath leaves the Carbost
road just beyond the Sligachan Hotel. A nearby
bridge crosses a stream and the footpath
crosses the moor towards the foot of Sgurr nan
Gillean's northern flank. Follow this path as far
as the Allt Dearg Beag. From here continue on
the west bank of the stream to a bridge. Cross
the stream and follow the path which heads in a
southerly direction. Continue into Coire
Riabhach past the lochan with the obvious wall
of the Pinnacle Ridge on your right. A long,
hard pull through a jumble of boulders
eventually gives access to the crest of the SE
ridge. The ridge is at first fairly broad, but
higher up it narrows considerably and you will
have to scramble the final few feet to the
summit of Sgurr nan Gillean. Descend the west
ridge steeply to the Tooth of Sgurr nan Gillean.
To the north of the Tooth a narrow cleft known
as Nicholson's Chimney offers an abseil route to
the base of the crag from where you can
contour across the screes to regain the ridge
east of Am Basteir. An easy but exposed
scramble leads to the summit. Descend to the
Bhasteir Tooth by way of ledges on the Lota
Corrie (south) side for 60 feet/18m. Here the
way down is made difficult by a small wall.
Either abseil or descend a difficult pitch of
about 20 feet/six metres down a slightly easier-
angled section of wall to the SE. From the foot
of the wall a sloping shelf and ramp leads to the
top of the Bhasteir Tooth. From here abseil

down the line of Naismith's Route to the
Bealach nan Lice, or alternatively, return to the
wall which you climbed earlier or abseiled
down, and follow a terrace which inclines down
towards Lota Corrie. Narrow shelves and walls
lead to wider ledges at the foot of the cliffs from
where you can climb screes up to the Bealach
nan Lice. From the bealach climb over Sgurr
a'Fionn Choire to reach Bruach na Frithe.
Descend by the NW ridge to the Bealach
a'Mhaim and Sligachan.

🦌 No restrictions.

BEN MORE (MULL), 3169FT/966M

Map: OS Sheet 48: GR 526331
Translation: big hill
Pronunciation: byn moar
Access Point: Loch na Keal, GR 506368
Distance/ascent: 8mls/3100ft; 13km/945m
Approx Time: 4-7 hours

🐾 Start at the foot of the Abhainn na h-Uamha
and follow the south bank up the grassy Gleann
na Beinne Fada to reach the col between Beinn
Fhada and A'Chioch. Turn south and climb
towards A'Chioch. Continue on the ridge over
A'Chioch to Ben More. Descend by the broad
NW ridge.

🦌 No number listed.

Recommended Books

Bennet, Donald (ed), *The Munros: the Scottish Mountaineering Club Hillwalkers' Guide*, Glasgow, Scottish Mountaineering Trust, 1985.

Brown, Hamish, *Hamish's Mountain Walk: the first traverse of all the Scottish Munros in one journey*, London, Gollancz, 1978.

Butterfield, Irvine, *The High Mountains of Britain and Ireland*, London, Diadem Books, 1986.

Gilbert, Richard, *Memorable Munros*, Leicester, Diadem Books, 1983.

Moran, Martin, *The Munros in Winter: 277 summits in 83 days*, Newton Abbot, David and Charles, 1986.

Mountaineering Council of Scotland and the Scottish Landowners' Federation (compilers), *Heading for the Scottish Hills*, Glasgow, Scottish Mountaineering Trust, 1988.

Munro's Tables of the 3000-feet mountains of Scotland and other tables of lesser heights, Revised edition, Edinburgh, Scottish Mountaineering Trust, 1984.

McNeish, Cameron, *The Corbett Almanac*, Neil Wilson Publishing , 1994.

Dempster, Andrew, *The Munro Phenomenon*, Mainstream Publishing, 1995.

Dawson, Alan, *The Relative Hills of Britain*, Cicerone, 1992.

Drummond Peter, *Scottish Hill and Mountain Names*, SMT, 1991.

Weather Information

West Highlands, Tel: 0891-112235
East Highlands, Tel: 0891-112236

INDEX OF MUNROS

Beinn Fhionnlaidh	3297ft/1005m	108
Beinn Ghlas	3619ft/1103m	26
Beinn Heasgarnich	3530ft/1076m	29
Beinn Ime	3316ft/1011m	12
Beinn Iutharn Mhor	3428ft/1045m	67
Beinn Liath Mhor	3035ft/925m	115
Beinn Liath Mhor Fannaich	3130ft/954m	125
Beinn Mhanach	3130ft/954m	32
Beinn Mheadhoin	3878ft/1182m	78
Beinn na Lap	3074ft/937m	55
Beinn nan Aighenan	3150ft/960m	36
Beinn Narnain	3038ft/926m	12
Beinn Sgritheall	3195ft/974m	96
Beinn Sgulaird	3074ft/937m	40
Beinn Tarsuinn	3071ft/936m	122
Beinn Teallach	3002ft/915m	88
Beinn Tulaichean	3104ft/946m	16
Beinn Udlamain	3314ft/1010m	62
Ben Alder	3766ft/1148m	58
Ben Avon (Leabaidh an Daimh Bhuidhe)	3842ft/1171m	83
Ben Chonzie	3054ft/931m	21
Ben Cruachan	3694ft/1126m	34
Ben Hope	3041ft/927m	131
Ben Klibreck	3153ft/961m	130
Ben Lawers	3983ft/1214m	26
Ben Lomond	3195ft/974m	12
Ben Lui	3707ft/1130m	18
Ben Macdui	4295ft/1309m	82
Ben More (Mull)	3169ft/966m	138
Ben More	3852ft/1174m	17
Ben More Assynt	3274ft/998m	130
Ben Nevis	4409ft/1344m	49
Ben Oss	3373ft/1028m	19
Ben Starav	3537ft/1078m	36
Ben Vane	3002ft/915m	13
Ben Vorlich	3094ft/943m	13
Ben Vorlich	3232ft/985m	20
Ben Wyvis (Glas Leathad Mor)	3432ft/1046m	126
Bidean nam Bian	3773ft/1150m	42
Bidein a'Choire Sheasgaich	3100ft/945m	115
Binnein Beag	3084ft/940m	46
Binnein Mor	3701ft/1128m	46
Bla Bheinn (Blaven)	3045ft/928m	133
Braeriach	4252ft/1296m	77
Braigh Coire Chruinn-bhalgain	3510ft/1070m	64
Broad Cairn	3274ft/998m	72
Bruach na Frithe	3143ft/958m	137
Buachaille Etive Beag (Stob Dubh)	3143ft/958m	42
Buachaille Etive Mor (Stob Dearg)	3353ft/1022m	41
Bynack More	3576ft/1090m	79
Cairn Bannoch	3320 ft/1012m	72
Cairn of Claise	3491ft/1064m	71
Cairn Toul	4242ft/1293m	80
Cairngorm	4085ft/1245m	78
Carn a'Chlamain	3159ft/963m	66
Carn a'Coire Bhoidheach	3668ft/1118m	72
Carn a'Gheoidh	3199ft/975m	68
Carn a'Mhaim	3402ft/1037m	82

Carn an Fhidhleir	3261ft/994m	66
Carn an Righ	3376ft/1029m	67
Carn an t-Sagairt Mor	3435ft/1047m	72
Carn an Tuirc	3343ft/1019m	71
Carn Aosda	3008ft/917m	68
Carn Bhac	3104ft/946m	67
Carn Dearg	3087ft/941m	55
Carn Dearg	3100ft/945m	86
Carn Dearg	3392ft/1034m	58
Carn Eige (Eighe)	3881ft/1183m	108
Carn Ghluasaid	3140ft/957m	103
Carn Gorm	3373ft/1028m	23
Carn Liath	3199ft/975m	64
Carn Liath	3300ft/1006m	87
Carn Mairg	3415ft/1041m	23
Carn Mor Dearg	4012ft/1223m	49
Carn na Caim	3087ft/941m	63
Carn nan Gabhar	3704ft/1129m	64
Carn nan Ghobhar	3255ft/992m	110
Carn nan Gobhar	3255ft/992m	109
Carn Sgulain	3018ft/920m	86
Chno Dearg	3435ft/1047m	54
Ciste Dhubh	3222ft/982m	102
Cona'Mheall	3215ft/980m	127
Conival	3238ft/987m	130
Creag a'Mhaim	3107ft/947m	100
Creag Leacach	3238ft/987m	70
Creag Meagaidh	3707ft/1130m	87
Creag Mhor	3218ft/981m	23
Creag Mhor	3438ft/1048m	29
Creag nan Damh	3012ft/918m	100
Creag Pitridh	3031ft/924m	59
Creise	3609ft/1100m	39
Cruach Ardrain	3431ft/1046m	16
Derry Cairngorm	3789ft/1155m	82
Driesh	3107ft/947m	74
Druim Shionnach	3238ft/987m	100
Eididh nan Clach Geala	3045ft/928m	127
Fionn Bheinn	3061ft/933m	116
Gairich	3015ft/919m	94
Garbh Chioch Mhor	3323ft/1013m	93
Geal Charn	3008ft/917m	62
Geal Charn	3038ft/926m	86
Geal Charn	3442ft/1049m	59
Geal Charn	3714ft/1132m	58
Glas Bheinn Mhor	3271ft/997m	36
Glas Maol	3504ft/1068m	70
Glas Tulaichean	3448ft/1051m	67
Gleouraich	3396ft/1035m	97
Gulvain	3238ft/987m	90
Inaccessible Pinnacle	3235ft/986m	134
Ladhar Bheinn	3346ft/1020m	96
Liathach	3458ft/1054m	118
Lochnagar	3789ft/1155m	73
Luinne Bheinn	3080ft/939m	95
Lurg Mhor	3235ft/986m	115
Mam Sodhail (Mam Soul)	3871ft/1180m	108
Maoile Lunndaidh	3304ft/1007m	113

Maol Chean-dearg	3061ft/933m	116
Maol Chinn-dearg	3218ft/981m	100
Mayar	3045ft/928m	74
Meall a'Bhuiridh	3635ft/1108m	39
Meall a'Choire Leith	3038ft/926m	25
Meall a'Chrasgaidh	3064ft/934m	125
Meall Buidhe	3058ft/932m	23
Meall Buidhe	3104ft/946m	95
Meall Chuaich	3120ft/951m	62
Meall Corranaich	3507ft/1069m	25
Meall Dearg	3127ft/953m	43
Meall Garbh	3176ft/968m	23
Meall Garbh	3668ft/1118m	26
Meall Ghaordie	3409ft/1039m	28
Meall Glas	3150ft/960m	30
Meall Gorm	3113ft/949m	125
Meall Greigh	3284ft/1001m	26
Meall na Teanga	3008ft/917m	90
Meall nan Ceapraichean	3205ft/977m	127
Meall nan Eun	3045ft/928m	38
Meall nan Tarmachan	3422ft/1043m	27
Monadh Mor	3651ft/1113m	82
Moruisg	3045ft/928m	113
Mount Keen	3081ft/939m	75
Mullach an Rathain	3356ft/1023m	118
Mullach Clach a'Bhlair	3343ft/1019m	77
Mullach Coire Mhic Fhearchair	3343ft/1019m	122
Mullach Fraoch-choire	3615ft/1102m	103
Mullach na Dheiragain	3222ft/982m	107
Mullach nan Coirean	3081ft/939m	48
Na Gruagaichean	3461ft/1055m	46
Ruadh Stac Mor	3012ft/918m	121
Sail Chaorainn	3287ft/1002m	103
Saileag	3146ft/959m	102
Schiehallion	3553ft/1083m	22
Seana Bhraigh	3041ft/927m	128
Sgairneach Mhor	3251ft/991m	62
Sgiath Chuil	3067ft/935m	30
Sgor an Iubhair	3286ft/1001m	46
Sgor Gaibhre	3133ft/955m	55
Sgor Gaoith	3668ft/1118m	77
Sgor na h-Ulaidh	3261ft/994m	40
Sgor nam Fiannaidh	3173ft/967m	43
Sgorr Dhearg	3360ft/1024m	44
Sgorr Dhonuill	3284ft/1001m	44
Sgorr Ruadh	3150ft/960m	115
Sgurr a'Bhealaich Dheirg	3405ft/1038m	102
Sgurr a'Chaorachain	3455ft/1053m	113
Sgurr a'Choire Ghlais	3553ft/1083m	110
Sgurr a'Chreadaidh	3192ft/973m	136
Sgurr a'Mhadaidh	3012ft/918m	136
Sgurr a'Mhaim	3606ft/1099m	46
Sgurr a'Mhaoraich	3369ft/1027m	97
Sgurr Alasdair	3258ft/993m	134
Sgurr an Doire Leathain	3314ft/1010m	100
Sgurr an Lochain	3294ft/1004m	100
Sgurr Ban	3245ft/989m	122
Sgurr Breac	3281ft/1000m	126

Sgurr Choinnich	3277ft/999m	113
Sgurr Choinnich Mor	3592ft/1095m	51
Sgurr Dubh Mor	3097ft/944m	133
Sgurr Eilde Mor	3307ft/1008m	46
Sgurr Fhuar-thuill	3441ft/1049m	110
Sgurr Fhuaran	3504ft/1068m	101
Sgurr Mhic Choinnich	3110ft/948m	134
Sgurr Mor	3290ft/1003m	94
Sgurr Mor	3645ft/1111m	125
Sgurr na Banachdich	3166ft/965m	136
Sgurr na Ciche	3415ft/1041m	93
Sgurr na Ciste Duibhe	3369ft/1027m	101
Sgurr na Lapaich	3772ft/1150m	109
Sgurr na Ruaidhe	3258ft/993m	110
Sgurr na Sgine	3100ft/945m	99
Sgurr nan Ceannaichean	3002ft/915m	113
Sgurr nan Ceathreamhnan	3776ft/1151m	107
Sgurr nan Clach Geala	3586ft/1093m	125
Sgurr nan Coireachan	3127ft/953m	94
Sgurr nan Coireachan	3136ft/956m	91
Sgurr nan Conbhairean	3642ft/1110m	103
Sgurr nan Each	3028ft/923m	125
Sgurr nan Eag	3037ft/924m	133
Sgurr nan Gillean	3166ft/965m	137
Sgurr Thuilm	3159ft/963m	91
Slioch	3215ft/980m	120
Spidean a'Choire Leith	3458ft/1054m	118
Spidean Mialach	3268ft/996m	97
Sron a'Choire Ghairbh	3067ft/935m	90
Stob a'Choire Mheadhoin	3629ft/1106m	52
Stob a'Choire Odhair	3094ft/943m	38
Stob Ban	3205ft/977m	51
Stob Ban	3277ft/999m	48
Stob Binnein	3822ft/1165m	17
Stob Choire a'Chairn	3218ft/981m	46
Stob Choire Claurigh	3861ft/1177m	51
Stob Coir'an Albannaich	3425ft/1044m	38
Stob Coire an Laoigh	3658ft/1115m	51
Stob Coire Easain	3661ft/1116m	52
Stob Coire Sgriodain	3202ft/976m	54
Stob Diamh	3274ft/998m	34
Stob Ghabhar	3566ft/1087m	38
Stob Poite Coire Ardair	3455ft/1053m	87
Stuc a'Chroin	3199ft/975m	20
Stuchd an Lochain	3150ft/960m	23
The Cairnwell	3061ft/933m	68
The Devil's Point	3294ft/1004m	80
The Saddle	3314ft/1010m	99
Toll Creagach	3458ft/1054m	108
Tolmount	3143ft/958m	71
Tom a'Choinich	3645ft/1111m	108
Tom Buidhe	3140ft/957m	71